D1474142

An Ancient Heritage

The Arab-American Minority

Young Muslims attending a youth retreat in Los Angeles.

An Ancient Heritage

The Arab-American Minority

BRENT ASHABRANNER

Photographs by Paul S. Conklin

HarperCollins*Publishers*

Photo credits: Courtesy of Naff Arab-American Collection, Archives Center, National Museum of American History, Smithsonian Institution, 25, 26, 33.

An Ancient Heritage: The Arab-American Minority
Text copyright © 1991 by Brent Ashabranner
Photographs copyright © 1991 by Paul Conklin
Printed in the United States of America. For information address HarperCollins Children's Books, a division of HarperCollins Publishers, 10 East 53rd Street, New York, NY 10022.
1   2   3   4   5   6   7   8   9   10
First Edition

Library of Congress Cataloging-in-Publication Data
Ashabranner, Brent, date
   An ancient heritage: the Arab-American minority / Brent
Ashabranner ; photographs by Paul S. Conklin.
      p.   cm.
   Includes bibliographical references.
   Summary: Discusses the cultural experience of Arab Americans and
the history of Arab immigration to the United States.
   ISBN 0-06-020048-0. — ISBN 0-06-020049-9 (lib. bdg.)
   1. Arab Americans—Juvenile literature.   [1. Arab Americans.]
I. Conklin, Paul, ill.   II. Title.
E184.A65A84   1991   90-30641
973'.04927—dc20   CIP
                                                                 AC

For Lamees Al-ayubi

Contents

1. A Little-Known American Minority   1
2. A Note on the Arabs and Arab History   10
3. Arab Americans: The Early Years   17
4. Arab Americans After World War II   35
5. "I Have This Longing"   62
6. Work   82
7. "Let Education Open a Door"   102
8. Growing Up Arab American   113
Bibliography   143
Index   145

I believe in you, and I believe in your destiny. I believe that you are contributors to this new civilization.

I believe that you have inherited from your forefathers an ancient dream, a song, a prophecy, which you can proudly lay as a gift of gratitude upon the lap of America.

—Kahlil Gibran, from a message to young Americans of Arabic descent

O N E

A Little-Known American Minority

Terry Ahwal lives with her mother and father in the Detroit suburb of Livonia. Terry and her family are Palestinian Arabs; they lived in the city of Ramallah in Israeli-occupied territory called the West Bank before coming to America during the 1970s. They all became American citizens as quickly as they could.

"We go to a Roman Catholic church here, just as we did in Ramallah," Terry told Paul and me the first time we met her. "We're very active in the church, but some people still ask us if we believe in Christ. They want to know if we celebrate Christmas. My goodness, Christmas was born in our part of the world."

*　　*　　*

1

The Reverend Father George Shalhoub is pastor of St. Mary's Antiochian Orthodox Church in Livonia. His parish is made up of five hundred families, all Arab American, who come from the entire western side of Detroit. Services at St. Mary's are mostly conducted in English, but Scriptures are read in both Arabic and English. Weddings are often in Arabic. St. Mary's is a pleasant church with lovely stained-glass windows, but it is not large.

"When everyone comes at once, we have chaos," Father George told us with a smile.

"When our church was in the planning stage, in 1974, there was quite a bit of opposition from people who live around here," Father George said. "One of our neighbors said, 'I don't want these Arabs to be my neighbors. I hear they dance all night.'

"But there is a tradition in America for people to be accepting once they know something about you. That is why we open up the church several times a year to let the community share our food, crafts, music, and dances. Now all our neighbors come. We have never resigned ourselves to being misunderstood and disliked!"

Anthony Shadid is a student at the University of Wisconsin, but I met him in Washington, D.C., when he was taking part in an Arab-American Anti-Discrimination Committee summer intern program. Tony was born and grew up in Oklahoma City, where his father is a dentist. Both his maternal and paternal grandparents came from Lebanon, but Tony said there was never any strong effort to preserve Arabic traditions in his family.

"Just lots of family gatherings," he said, "and lots of good Lebanese food. We never tried to hide our background, but I was just like any other kid in school. Some had Irish or Italian backgrounds. Mine was Lebanese."

But on the subject of prejudice, Tony did have memories. "Once in a while in school there was some name calling—'camel jockey,' stuff like that. Especially when the Iranians took the American hostages."

"But Iranians aren't Arabs," I said.

"Most people don't know that," Tony said, "or don't care. We get lumped together."

"What other names were you called?" I asked.

" 'Sand nigger,' " he said, "once or twice."

As he has grown older, Tony's interest in his roots, his Arabic heritage, has also grown. He is studying journalism in college and wants to focus on Middle Eastern affairs.

Casey Kasem is America's most famous disc jockey. For years, his immensely popular radio show, *American Top 40,* and his equally popular television show, *Amer-*

Casey Kasem

ica's Top 10, have been listened to and watched by millions of people every week in this country and around the world. Recently he left ABC's *American Top 40* to produce his own show, *Casey's Top 40.* To his fans Casey is simply America's deejay.

He is also an Arab American, born of Lebanese parents in Detroit in 1932. I talked to Casey about his Arab background one morning as I rode with him to a Beverly Hills studio where he was scheduled to tape an *America's Top 10* show.

Casey Kasem preparing to host an *America's Top 10* program.

"My father was one of the hardest-working men I ever knew," Casey said. "He was only a boy when he left Lebanon, and he worked as a peddler with a pack on his back in Mexico. He was just fourteen when he came to America and went to work for the railroad in Tyrone, Pennsylvania. Later he opened his first grocery store in Detroit on Brush Street near Harper Hospital, where I was born. He and my mother worked there every day from morning to night.

"My father couldn't read or write in any language, but it wasn't long before he was completely Americanized. He loved baseball, the Detroit Tigers. This was his country. But he never forgot his roots. I grew up listening to Arab music, and I still love it. My family and their friends got together a lot for Arab dancing. All of that is still in my blood. I was taught to be proud of our heritage.

"I'm an American, but I let people know about my Lebanese background. Arab Americans are a part of the ethnic quilt that Jesse Jackson talks about, just like blacks and Hispanics, Indians and Asians, but the media has painted a terrible pictures of Arabs—nothing but greedy oil billionaires, terrorists, playboy sheiks, and rug peddlers. That image rubs off on Arab Americans. I want to help change that."

Casey reeled off a string of names, most of them

6

famous or at least well known: F. Murray Abraham, Oscar winner for *Amadeus*; Doug Flutie, NFL quarterback and Heisman Trophy winner; Dr. Michael De-Bakey, world-renowned pioneer in open-heart surgery; Candy Lightner, who founded Mothers Against Drunk Driving; Danny Thomas, comedian and humanitarian; Senate Majority Leader George Mitchell of Maine; John Sununu, former Governor of New Hampshire, now President George Bush's chief of staff; Ralph Nader, consumer advocate; Christa McAuliffe, teacher and astronaut, lost aboard the space shuttle *Challenger*.

"They're all Arab Americans," Casey said. "How many people know that?"

As Casey drove his Mercedes effortlessly over the crowded Los Angeles freeway, our talk jumped back and forth between Arab Americans and music, which has been so much a part of his life. At one point Casey said, "If people don't understand something, they usually hate it. When they understand it, their prejudice usually disappears."

"Are you talking about people getting to know Arab Americans?" I asked.

Casey laughed. "I was talking about rock and roll," he said. "But the same thing applies to Arab Americans, doesn't it?"

*   *   *

No one knows with certainty how many Arab Americans—Arab immigrants and their descendants born in America—live in the United States today. The best-informed estimates put the number at two and a half million, with the reservation that the actual number may vary by half a million on either side of that figure. One reason a more precise total for Arab Americans cannot be arrived at is that early immigration records often listed Arabs as Turks. Another reason is that Arabs who go first to non-Arab countries and then immigrate to the United States are listed by the nationality of the last country they lived in.

But whether the correct figure is two, two and a half, or three million, Arab Americans form an important ethnic minority in the United States today: about half the size of the Jewish population of the country, for example, and much larger than the total population of American Indians. Yet of all American ethnic groups of substantial size, Arab Americans probably are the least known and least understood by other Americans.

Who are the people who make up the Arab-American ethnic minority in the United States today? Where do they live? What do they do? What special problems do they have? What do they want to achieve? What are their contributions to this country? Those were some of the questions that Paul and I wanted to answer in this book.

We think we found those answers and more. We know we learned a great deal about a people who are a part of the "American quilt." But to better understand today's Arab Americans, we first need to look briefly at Arab history and at early Arab immigration to America.

T W O

A Note on the Arabs
and Arab History

The Arab people originated thousands of years ago as a number of nomadic tribes in the desert area of western Asia known today as the Arabian Peninsula. Like the Jews, they traced their ancestry to Abraham and Shem, the eldest of Noah's three sons. The early Arabs were pastoralists, herding their sheep, goats, and camels through the harsh desert terrain; the search for water and edible brush for their animals never ended.

This stern and unforgiving environment fostered the qualities that are to this day associated with the Arab character: closeness of the family and clan, for mutual support was necessary to survival; submission of individual ambition to group welfare; personal honor in keeping one's word; a capacity for the hard work necessary to wrest a living from endless sand; hospitality to anyone who needed help in the desert, even an enemy (in contrast, also unrelenting hatred of an enemy—the desert provided no natural defenses, and a man's best defense of family and clan was his courage and fighting heart).

In time, some Arabs settled around oases and began cultivating dates, grains, and other crops. The Arabian Peninsula became a crossroads for caravans carrying spices, ivory, and other goods from southern Arabia and Africa to civilizations in the north. The oasis settlements became trading centers and grew into cities. Still, the Arab ideal remained the bedouin, the pastoral wanderer for whom the desert, with all its dangers and privations, meant freedom.

The seventh century A.D. marked a momentous turning point in Arab history. In the city of Mecca, probably in the year 571, a son was born to an Arab merchant, whose name was Abdullah; he was of the Hashim clan of the Quraysh tribe. Abdullah named his son Muhammad.

Little of historic fact is known about Muhammad's early life, but it is certain that he was a man of intense spiritual feelings. He thought deeply about the Arab polytheistic beliefs of his time, and his travels as a merchant and trader brought him in contact with both Christianity and Judaism. In midlife he often secluded himself in a cave in the hills near Mecca to meditate. Tradition holds that Muhammad was visited in the cave one night by the archangel Gabriel, who revealed to him the true word of God. After this experience, Muhammad became the prophet and founder of a new religion, Islam, which means "submission to God's will."

The new religion was in many ways related to Christianity and Judaism, both monotheistic religions (believing in a single God). The same God is worshiped in all three religions. Indeed, in Islamic belief Muhammad is the last and greatest in a long succession of prophets that includes Abraham, Moses, and Jesus.

The dominant message of Islam was total submission to an all-powerful but compassionate God. (The Arabic word for God is Allah.) The followers of the new religion were called Muslims, which in Arabic means "one who submits." Muhammad's teachings, based on Allah's revelations to him, were set down in Arabic and make up the holy book of the Muslims, the Koran.

During the early years of the seventh century, Muhammad preached to the tribes of the Arabian peninsula his message of submission to an all-powerful God, and the clear, straightforward teachings of Islam found ready reception in the Arab nature. In a remarkably short time Islam was firmly established as the religion of the Arabs.

With a speed equally remarkable, Muhammad's successors, after his death in 632, carried the word of Allah northward to other parts of western Asia, eastward to Persia, Afghanistan, and India. They entrenched Islam throughout North Africa from Egypt on the Red Sea to Morocco on the Atlantic coast. They gained a European foothold for the new religion in Spain. Under the banner of Islam, a few loosely related Arab tribes created a great empire.

The years between the seventh and the thirteenth centuries have been called the Golden Age of Arab civilization. Great Arab cities—Baghdad, Damascus, Cairo, Timbuktu, Fez, Granada, Córdoba—became centers of intellectual achievement. Universities were built, splendid libraries established. The best scholars from India, Persia, Greece, and other countries were brought to Baghdad—the center of the Arab world—and other Arab learning centers to share their knowledge and add to the development of Arab culture.

Arab contributions to human knowledge during the Golden Age were enormous. Arab mathematicians improved on the Hindu concept of zero, developed the systems of algebra, geometry, and trigonometry, and carried them to Europe. The science of astronomy was advanced at the great observatories at Palmyra and Maragha. Arab astronomers established longitude and latitude, investigated the speeds of sound and light, and explored the possibility that the earth rotated on its own axis. Some of the most famous medical authorities of the Middle Ages were Arabs. Advances in architecture, agriculture, navigation, geography, and the recording of world history resulted from Arab industry and genius during this period.

The richness of the Arabic language grew with these developments. Hundreds of English words have their roots in the Arabic language. A list of just a few of them indicates the many connections between the Arab past and our present: admiral, alfalfa, almanac, average, calendar, candy, coffee, cotton, gauze, jar, magazine, racquet, satin, sherbet, sugar, traffic, zero.

But the greatness of the Golden Age was not to last. By the thirteenth century the Arab Empire was weakening through internal political strife. The Arabs were forced out of Spain. Mongol and Turkish invasions from the north brought great destruction to Arab lands and ruin to the major cities. Outlying provinces in North Africa broke free of the rule of Damascus authority. By the sixteenth century the Ottoman Turkish Empire had established its sovereignty over much of what had been the Arab Empire. After World War I Great Britain and France, in an exercise of traditional colonialism, divided most of the old Ottoman Empire between them, making subject states of most Arab countries. Only Saudi Arabia, the original homeland of the Arabs, remained free of European colonialism.

During their centuries of expansion, the Arabs carried Islam to many parts of the world and implanted in these places other elements of Arab culture. But in most cases, the countries and people that embraced Islam retained their own languages and cultures that made them a distinct people. That was true of the people of Persia (Iran), Byzantium (Turkey), Afghanistan, Central Asia, Indonesia, East Africa, and other parts of the world. They became Muslims but not Arabs.

On the other hand, many people not only adopted the religion of the prophet Muhammad but in a relatively short period of history became speakers of Arabic and absorbed the customs, values, and traditions of the Arabs. That was true of the people of much of southwest Asia. It was true of the Egyptians and other North African people, the ancestors of modern Libyans, Tunisians, Algerians, Moroccans, and Sudanese. It was in this vast area of Asia and Africa that a common Arab culture emerged.

Who then are the Arabs of today? They are people who speak Arabic as a native language. Most are Muslims, though a tiny minority (five or six percent) are Christians. They follow the customs and believe in the values and traditions of their Arab ancestors. Most important, they think of themselves as Arabs.

THREE

Arab Americans: The Early Years

Some books have their beginnings in unexpected ways. I could not have known it then, but the seed of this book about Arab Americans was planted in my head half a century ago when I was growing up in a small town in Creek County, Oklahoma. The town was Bristow, a farming community of five thousand that was also on the edge of oil-well activity in that part of the state. Even during the Depression, Bristow was a good, relatively prosperous place to grow up.

I moved to Bristow with my parents when I was twelve. When I started seventh grade, I discovered that some of my classmates, several of whom quickly became friends, had surnames that sounded strange to my Mid-western ear—names such as Naifeh, Horani, Shibley, and Khoury. Other last names had a biblical ring to them: Abraham and Joseph. Most of the boys and girls with these names had light-brown skin not unlike that of the few Mexicans I had seen in my life.

But my new classmates and friends weren't Mexicans. Their parents or grandparents, I soon learned, had come from a country called Syria. I had never heard of Syria, but when I located it on a world map, I discovered some names that were familiar: Palestine, which bordered Syria, and Jerusalem and Bethlehem, cities in Palestine. Little by little I pieced together the story of how these Arab families, which had their beginnings in Syria, came to be a substantial part of the population of a small town in Oklahoma.

An immigrant peddler named Joseph Abraham look-ing for new customers for his wares—mostly clothes and canned food—reached Bristow, which was still In-dian territory in 1899. The discovery of oil was bringing large numbers of people to Bristow and other towns in the area, and the kinds of things Abraham had to sell were in great demand. He settled in Bristow and reg-ularly received replenishments of goods from his backer and supplier in the East. His life as a roving peddler was over. He became a successful merchant, an investor in cotton and real estate, and in time a man of great economic power in Oklahoma when it emerged as a state.

Joe Abraham, as he was called by everyone in Bristow, brought his relatives from Syria and urged his friends to come. His relatives and friends encouraged their friends to immigrate and settle in Bristow. They went into business mostly. Ed Abraham had a grocery store; the Shibley family opened a cafe; the Horanis ran a filling station; others went into the clothing business; and several worked for Joe Abraham. By the time I moved to Bristow in 1934, Syrian Americans—including children who had been born in Bristow—numbered several hundred.

Although some of their parents, and especially grand-parents, spoke English with an accent, the Syrian-American kids I went through junior high and high school with did not. They may have understood some Arabic, but I never heard them speak it. They were as thoroughly Americanized as I or any of my Anglo-Saxon friends were. I played golf with Ed Naifeh. I went on Boy Scout trips with Malik Khoury. I wrote stories for the high school paper about Warren Shibley's accomplishments on the football and basketball teams.

I did see differences between us. Their families were large and close-knit, and they seemed to work together in family businesses. The difference that meant most to me then, I suppose, was their food. I grew to love Syrian food, as most people in Bristow called it, and I wangled every invitation I could to have dinner at my Syrian-American friends' houses. The food might be plain Oklahoma fare, but more likely the dinner table would be loaded with *kibbeh*—a meat patty with pine nuts—stuffed chicken called *djaaj mahshi,* vine leaf rolls, cabbage rolls, green bean stew, and bowls of *hummus*—a delicious chickpea spread—with stacks of round unleavened bread. If I was lucky, there would be *baklawa* for dessert and sometimes, around Easter, cookies called *ma'amoul.* If I had gone very long without an invitation, I talked my parents into eating out at Shibley's cafe where once a week, on Thursday nights, they served Syrian food.

But the differences between us were few. There was not even a religious difference. I think all the Syrian-American families were Christian; most were Catholic, but a few were Protestant. I knew a little about Islam even in those days because I had devoured *Beau Geste, Beau Sabreur,* and *Beau Ideal,* P. C. Wren's exciting novels about the French Foreign Legion in Arab North Africa. But if there was even a single Muslim among the Syrian Americans in Bristow, I never heard about him.

Later in life I lived and worked with many Arabs—Libyans, Egyptians, Lebanese, Palestinians—in North Africa and the Middle East; those experiences are doubtless also a part of the reason I wanted to write this book.

20

But I still think the root of the reason goes back to kids like Ed Naifeh and Paul Joseph whom I grew up with in Oklahoma. They came out of an Arab background, but they were as American as anybody I ever knew.

Arabs began coming to America in the last decades of the nineteenth century. They came in a trickle of a few thousand a year compared with the flood of millions of Europeans who immigrated to America during the late 1800s and early 1900s, but the stream of Arab immigrants was a steady one throughout the first quarter of the twentieth century.

The great majority of these Arab immigrants came from one small area of the Middle East: a stretch of land at the eastern end of the Mediterranean Sea that was in those days a district of Syria known as Mount Lebanon, but is today the Republic of Lebanon. This is mountainous country, with two main ranges paralleling the coast. The range in the west is called the Lebanon; the range in the east is called the Anti-Lebanon. Between these ranges lies a fertile agricultural valley that for centuries has been known as Al Biqa. The valley is noted for its grains, olives, and citrus fruits.

According to Phillip K. Hitti, a distinguished Arab historian, the inhabitants of this region are descendants of Phoenician-Canaanite tribes who came to the area more than two thousand years before Christ. Like so many other peoples after the rise and spread of Islam during the seventh century, they became speakers of Arabic and absorbed Arab values, traits, and traditions. Before its independence in 1945, Lebanon was politically a part of Syria, but the people of this region of mountain, valley, and coastal plain thought of themselves as separate and had little attachment to the Syrian government. They had even less regard for the Ottoman Turk rulers who held sovereignty over Syria and other Arab countries from the sixteenth century until after World War I. The loyalties that the Mount Lebanon people felt were primarily those that had dominated Arab society from early times: loyalty to immediate family, to extended family, to village, to religious group.

Another important characteristic of Lebanon is that it has long been a place of great religious diversity. For centuries, Christians and Muslims existed there side by side in approximately equal numbers (now there is a Muslim majority). Most of the Christians are Maronites but there are substantial numbers of Melkites; both groups consider themselves to be part of the Roman Catholic Church. Most of the remaining Christians are members of the Eastern or Antiochian Orthodox Church. The Muslim population is split between the Sunnite and Shiite sects; the two sects are in historic disagreement about the rightful successor to Muhammad. Another religious group in Lebanon are the Druze, whose beliefs are essentially those of Islam but incorporate elements of other Eastern religions. Until recent times these diverse religious groups have lived together in Lebanon in relative peace.

There are several reasons why Syrians of Mount Lebanon made up the bulk of early Arab immigrants to America. Stories about economic opportunity in America and knowledge of the millions of European immigrants to the New World doubtless reached Mount Lebanon through the important Mediterranean port city of Beirut. Secondly, the Ottoman sultan of the time called upon his Arab subjects to exhibit their arts and crafts at the Philadelphia Centennial Exposition in 1876; this exhibition, a forerunner of later world's fairs, was a celebration of the first hundred years of United States independence. Some Christian Syrian-Lebanese merchants and artisans responded to the sultan's call; they brought back their own glowing stories about life in America and the opportunities for making one's fortune there.

The Mount Lebanon residents who made up the vanguard of Arab immigrants to America during the 1800s were almost all Christians. They knew America to be a predominantly Christian country and probably had less hesitation about venturing into the new and unknown land than did Muslim Arabs. In time Christian Arabs from other parts of Syria and Palestine immigrated to

America, as did some Muslim Arabs. But during the period between 1880 and 1925, almost ninety percent of the Arab immigrants were Christians, and nine out of ten of those came from Mount Lebanon.

The Arabs who came to America in the early period of immigration from the Middle East came for essentially the same reasons that motivated European immigrants during the same years. In almost all cases the Arabs were poor. They saw in America the prospect of economic opportunity and hope of a better life. Many planned to stay only a few years in America, make a great deal of money, then return to their villages in Lebanon to live the rest of their lives.

Most of the Arab immigrants to America were young men, the average age about twenty-four. Six out of ten were single, and of those married, only a few took their wives on their first trip. Some returned to Mount Lebanon and brought their wives and families back to America; some sent for them. Some of the young un-married men did return to their villages, but in almost all cases their stay was a short one. Life in the village was dull compared with what they had found in America. They soon returned, and often other young family mem-bers and friends—and sometimes brides—returned with them. Beginning in the mid-1890s the number of Arab women immigrants to America increased, though they never equaled the number of male immigrants.

But wherever they settled, most immigrants from Mount Lebanon preferred to work in the field of trade, and they first became peddlers of all kinds of merchandise: canned food, clothes, dishes, pots and pans, needles and thread, toys, tools—anything small enough to be carried in a wagon or a backpack and that people living on farms or in relatively isolated rural communities might need. The "Persian" peddler in the musical *Oklahoma!* was really a Syrian, and he was no figment of Richard Rodgers' and Oscar Hammerstein's imaginations. Such itinerant Arab tradesmen became a familiar and welcome tradition throughout rural America in the late nineteenth and early twentieth centuries.

William Aossy, Sr., a Syrian peddler in Urbana, Iowa, shown here with his truck, was one of many Arabs who took their merchandise into the countryside. Later many of these peddlers started stores across the Midwest.

Khalil Mikwee was an early Syrian back peddler, who took his merchandise into the countryside around Birmingham, Alabama.

26

The Syrian-Lebanese immigrant usually got his start as a peddler through the help of a countryman—often a family member or a friend—who had already established himself as a seller, supplier, or even manufacturer, of the kind of merchandise needed in the peddler's trade. The newly arrived immigrant peddler worked long hours seven days a week and saved his money. After a few years of working on commission or of borrowing and repaying, he had accumulated enough capital to go into business for himself. In time, he usually graduated from peddler to store owner, often beginning with a

Vigorous ninety-one-year-old Kadar Joseph lives in Albuquerque. He immigrated from Palestine in 1920; he peddled clothing in Colorado and later owned several stores there. Photo by David Conklin.

Rasmie Hindi, an immigrant from Beirut, who settled in rural New Mexico when she was twenty-one, sits with her son, Moneer, a retired space industry engineer, in their Albuquerque home. Between them is a photograph of Mrs. Hindi's husband, who was one of the earliest peddlers in the American southwest. Photo by David Conklin.

Rasmie Hindi.
Photo by David Conklin.

28

small grocery. Sometimes, from such modest beginnings, he went on to become a wealthy businessman.

Historians have no clear answer as to why so many of the early Syrian-Lebanese immigrants became peddlers. It is clear, however, that they did not see agriculture as the way to success in their new country. Peddling was a trade that did not require any special training. Neither did it require much money—in most cases the goods could be got on credit—and there were almost no overhead costs.

Whatever its attractions, the peddling trade had some important advantages in helping Arab immigrants adjust quickly to American life. In order to sell merchandise, they had to acquire a working knowledge of English in a hurry. And traveling around the country, dealing every day with native-born Americans, learning their customs and values, was an excellent way for them to become Americans themselves. Arab-American families who date their beginnings in America from the late nineteenth and early twentieth centuries almost without exception have one or more peddlers in their family tree.

My dentist for many years has been Dr. Wadie Courie, who practices in the Washington, D.C., suburb of Bethesda, Maryland. With six-month check-ups and an occasional filling, we have had time over two decades to talk about his family history. His father, Alexander

Wadie Courie with a patient.

Courie, was born in the village of Souk el Gharb in Mount Lebanon. At age seventeen—in 1910—he was brought to America by a brother who had been a peddler before establishing a grocery store in Kinston, North Carolina.

"I've seen the store," Dr. Courie told me. "It was called Courie's Cash Grocery."

His father became a peddler, taking merchandise from the grocery store on credit and paying for it after a selling trip. Walking the country roads of North Carolina with a pack on his back, sleeping in farmers' barns, was a hard but sure way for the young man from Mount Lebanon to get to know his new country. In time he graduated to a clerk's position in the Kinston grocery store and, when he was thirty-one, married a young

30

Lebanese woman whose family lived in Washington, D.C.

"My father heard that there were a lot of Lebanese families in Washington, D.C.," Dr. Courie said, "and he went there for the express purpose of finding a wife. My father belonged to the Syrian Orthodox Church. He got the priest in Washington to arrange for him to meet a marriage-aged girl. That meeting didn't work, but then my father met the girl's sister. That did work. They got married. My mother had come to the U.S. from Mount Lebanon when she was thirteen."

Alexander Courie and his wife lived in Kinston and Washington, D.C., for several years and then opened a grocery store in Detroit. They received financial help from one of Courie's brothers who had put himself through medical school at the University of Virginia and then begun practicing in Detroit. Wadie Courie was born in Detroit. He remembers that his father and mother both worked long hours in the store seven days a week to make a success of it. They wanted Wadie to go to Sunday school but had no time to take him to the Orthodox Church, which was in another part of the city. So he started going to the nearby Presbyterian Church.

When Wadie was ten years old his mother and father moved back to Washington, D.C., and started a grocery there. His mother did not like the cold Detroit winters. Wadie recalls that his mother and father usually spoke Arabic to each other but never to him or his two brothers. To the children, they spoke only English.

"They wanted us to be Americans," Dr. Courie said, "and one way was to confine our language to English. My mother cooked Lebanese food, but otherwise having a Lebanese background wasn't much of a factor in my life. There were a lot of ethnic kids in my school. If anyone thought about my background, they probably thought I was Italian or Jewish."

But, typical of almost all Lebanese immigrants, Alexander Courie insisted that his sons get good educations. "If you don't use your brain," he told them, doubtless remembering his years as a peddler, "you're going to have to use your feet."

One of Dr. Courie's brothers became a federal government civil servant, the other a medical doctor.

Wadie Courie served in the Air Force Medical Corps during the Korean War. He married a woman with a Pennsylvania German background and joined the Lutheran Church, of which she was a member. He regrets that he has never visited Lebanon.

"Obviously," Dr. Courie said to me once, "I didn't keep much of my Lebanese heritage."

In fact, the Couries were not unlike many, perhaps most, early Arab families in America. The prime concern of the first Syrian-Lebanese immigrants was to succeed in their new country. They saw quickly enough that

one way to do that was to reduce the differences between themselves and native-born Americans. Learning
English well was of utmost importance. Seeing that their
children got good educations was just as important. Because so many first-generation Arab Americans were
peddlers, they, and later their families, were scattered
all over the country, often in small communities like
Kinston, North Carolina, and Bristow, Oklahoma. Becoming American was simply easier in places such as
those than in big-city ghettos made up mainly of immigrants. Even when first-generation parents and grandparents tried to preserve Arab traditions in their

Nazina Micola, with her husband (left), brother-in-law (right), and two sons,
poses in Bismarck, North Dakota. The picture was taken before World War I.
The Micolas were Syrian.

families, their children and grandchildren usually retained only those that they could adapt easily to their lives as Americans.

A new immigration law passed by the U.S. Congress in 1924 placed severe limits on the numbers of persons who could immigrate to the United States except from northern and western European countries. The purpose of this highly discriminatory legislation was to maintain the "ethnic balance" of the United States as it was at that time. Most Americans in 1924, as today, could trace their ancestry to northern and western European countries—especially England, Ireland, and Germany—and a quota system established by the new law was to insure that this would continue to be the case. The law limited immigrants from Syria to one hundred per year!

The sharply curtailed Arab immigration after 1924 contributed further to weakening Arab-American ties to their original culture. Of necessity, Arab Americans increasingly associated with non-Arabs and married persons of non-Arabic backgrounds. During the 1930s and 1940s it seemed that Arab Americans might become so immersed in American life—so completely Americanized—that they would cease to exist as an ethnic minority.

But immigration laws change, and momentous world events that would alter the picture completely were on the horizon.

F O U R

Arab Americans After World War II

One of the historic outcomes of World War II was the determination of the colonial countries of Africa and Asia to gain their independence from European powers. The Arab countries threw off British and French rule, although France clung tenaciously to Algeria, its principal North African possession, until 1962. Seventeen independent Arab countries,* today often called the Arab world, have emerged since World War II. They cover 4.6 million square miles in western Asia and

---

*Algeria, Bahrain, Egypt, Iraq, Jordan, Kuwait, Lebanon, Libya, Morocco, Oman, Qatar, Saudi Arabia (never under colonial rule), Sudan, Syria, Tunisia, United Arab Emirates, Yemen. The countries of Djibouti, Mauritania, and Somalia are sometimes also included in a definition of the Arab world.

North Africa, an area about a million square miles larger than the United States. The total population of the countries is approximately 255 million, which is very close to the number of people who live in the United States.

Variation in size and population of the Arab countries is great. Sudan, with almost a million square miles, is larger than Alaska and Texas combined. On the other hand, Bahrain, Kuwait, Qatar, and the United Arab Emirates together would fit comfortably within the borders of Pennsylvania. Egypt, with 53 million people, is by far the most populous Arab country. Qatar, with less than half a million, is at the other end of the scale.

The most traumatic development in the post-World War II Arab world was the creation of the Jewish state of Israel out of Arab land that had been known for centuries as Palestine. Israel was born out of a dream of Jews throughout the world to return to the land of their biblical forefathers who had lived in kingdoms called Israel and Judah. From the time of the fall of Jerusalem to Roman armies in A.D. 70, not many Jews had lived in that ancient city or in Palestine until they began to return in increasing numbers in the late nineteenth century and after World War I. Following the holocaust of World War II still larger numbers of Jews returned to Palestine, and political pressures for the creation of a Jewish homeland were intensified.

In November 1947, the United Nations General Assembly approved a resolution to divide Palestine, then under British mandate, into a Jewish state and a Palestinian Arab state, with Jerusalem to become an international city under U.N. administration. The Jews accepted the division proposed by the U.N., but the Arab countries, particularly the neighboring countries of Lebanon, Syria, Jordan, Egypt, and Iraq, bitterly rejected not only the partition but also the concept of an independent Jewish state in their midst. It should be noted that in 1947 Jews made up thirty-two percent of the population of Palestine and owned eight percent of the land.

Six months after the U.N. resolution, the British withdrew from Palestine, and on May 14, 1948, the Jews proclaimed the state of Israel. For Palestinian Arabs in the newly proclaimed Jewish state there followed a period of uncertainty, fear, and panic. Fighting broke out on several fronts and in a number of cities. About 150,000 Palestinians elected to remain in Israel and become citizens of the new country. But between 600,000 and 700,000 Arabs fled from Israel or were expelled. The question of whether the Arabs who fled did so of their own choice (either from fear or refusal to live in a Jewish state) or whether they were forced out by Israelis has never been fully answered. Most recent studies strongly suggest that it was not a case entirely of one or the other: Many Palestinians left Israel voluntarily; others were forced to leave.

Since 1947 several bitter wars have been fought between Arab armies and Israel. In 1949, after heavy fighting, Jerusalem was divided between Israel and the Arab country of Jordan. The Old City in the east went to Jordan. Israel controlled the newer part of the city in the west.

Many Palestinians who fled from Israel immigrated to other countries. Most, however, have spent their lives in refugee camps in Jordan and Lebanon. They have raised their children there, many of whom—still living in these camps—now have children of their own.

The creation of Israel and the unresolved Palestinian refugee problem fostered an Arab nationalism and a sense of Arab unity that had never existed in the past. At the same time religious and political problems—in part related to Israel and demands for a Palestinian homeland—have created unrest and tension throughout the Arab world.

Lebanon, a country with a population about fifty-five percent Muslim and forty-five percent Christian, was under French mandate from the end of World War I until its independence was granted in 1943. Since 1975 a terrible civil war has raged in Lebanon. On one level it is a struggle between Muslims and Christians for political power, but there are many other bewildering aspects to the chaos in the country. Shia Muslims are fighting Sunni Muslims. Fifty thousand Syrian troops are in Lebanon, purportedly to keep peace but in fact adding to the violence. Large numbers of Palestinian refugees exist inside Lebanon. Israel has stationed troops inside the country in an area the Israelis declared a security zone. Conservatives and radicals within Lebanon's seventeen religious sects further fuel the unstable and violent situation. Since the civil war began, an estimated 150,000 people have been killed in the fighting. In a state of shock, dismembered by religious and political groups, Lebanon is today a country in name only.

Since the dramatic increase in oil prices during the 1970s, the Arab world has grown in international influence and importance. Some of the countries with immense oil production and reserves have become fabulously rich. The annual per-capita income of Kuwait and the United Arab Emirates is $24,000; of Qatar, an amazing $42,000, three times greater than the U.S. per-capita income. These figures are extreme, but the per-capita income of other oil-producing Arab countries is greater than the world average: Saudi Arabia, $11,000; Bahrain, $9,000; Libya, $6,000. Conversely, most Arab countries without oil as a natural resource are poverty-stricken and have meager per-capita incomes. Examples:

Syria, $700; Egypt, $560; Sudan, $370. This disparity in national wealth adds further to tensions in the Arab world.

World War II brought the United States into a closer relationship with the rest of the world, and it changed the way Americans looked at other countries and people. After the war many Americans began to question the racism and prejudice against certain nationalities that had become a part of U.S. immigration policy. President Eisenhower urged changes in immigration law to "get the bigotry out of it." President Kennedy said that quotas based on race and country of origin were "without basis in either logic or reason."

In 1965 a major new immigration law brought such racial and ethnic quota restrictions to an end. The number of immigrants allowed into the United States continued to be limited but in ways quite different from the past. Although some changes have been made in the 1965 landmark law—particularly in penalties for hiring illegal aliens—it is the basis for the present law.

The main feature of the 1965 immigration law is that no person can be refused immigrant status to the United States because of race or nationality. Special consideration is given to family reunification as a reason for immigration—children, brothers, sisters joining family members already in the United States. Preference is given to prospective immigrants with special occupational and professional skills that would be useful in the United States. The law also creates a special category—up to fifty thousand immigrants a year—for refugees from political or religious persecution.

Even since revision of the immigration law, immigration to America from Arab countries has been small when compared with the numbers of persons coming from south and southeast Asia and from Latin America. Since 1970 Mexico has been the leading country of origin for legal immigrants to the United States, followed by the Philippines, Korea, Cuba, India, and China. With the fall of South Vietnam to Communist North Vietnam in 1975, an outpouring of refugees greatly increased the number of Southeast Asians coming to America.

Nevertheless, Arab immigration to America has increased dramatically over that of the late nineteenth and early twentieth centuries. Since 1970, more than ten thousand people have arrived from the Middle East every year to begin new lives in this country. In some ways today's Arab immigrants are the same as those who came to America fifty to a hundred years ago. Many of the post-World War II immigrants come primarily for economic reasons: to seek the jobs and money-making

41

opportunities that this country offers. Some plan to stay only a few years but end up making the United States their home.

But, unlike their predecessors, most of today's immigrants from the Middle East arrive in America with good educations or for the purpose of getting more education. And, also unlike early immigrants, thousands of today's immigrants—particularly Palestinians and Lebanese—are leaving the Middle East (or not returning after study) because of the violence and political problems there. Many retain strong attachments to their country of origin and to Arab culture, and most feel strongly that the Palestinians are entitled to their own homeland. While ninety percent of early Arab immigrants were Christian, the large majority of those immigrating today are Muslim.

Although Arab Americans live in all parts of the United States, including small towns and rural areas, the majority today make their homes in large cities and surrounding metropolitan areas. Some cities such as Boston, Chicago, New York, and Los Angeles have Arab-American populations exceeding one hundred thousand. Almost fifty thousand live in and around San Francisco. And while most Arab Americans have settled in the northeastern part of the country, cities such as Houston, Texas; Jacksonville, Florida; and

Phoenix, Arizona, each have more than twenty thousand Arab-American residents.

But the largest number of Arab Americans, over two hundred thousand, live in Detroit, in the adjoining city of Dearborn, and in the surrounding suburbs. Arab immigrants began coming to Detroit in increasing numbers early in the twentieth century, drawn by job opportunities in the rapidly expanding automotive industry. They also found the location a fertile one in which to start small shops and stores—an extension of the peddler tradition. Today more than one thousand small food or

Riad Shatila ships Arab sweets from his Detroit bakery all over the United States. He is Lebanese.

Joseph George, who was born in northern Lebanon, came to Detroit in 1958. For years he has run a grocery store that has shelves filled with a great assortment of goods from his native land.

convenience stores—the local name is party store—in the greater Detroit area are owned and run by Arab Americans.

Most of the first arrivals in Detroit from the Middle East were Syrian-Lebanese; today Lebanese, numbering at least a hundred thousand, make up almost half of the Arab-American population of greater Detroit. Palestinians began to come to the area during the early 1920s, and their numbers have expanded dramatically since the

44

loss of their homeland and the creation of Israel in 1948. Iraq and Yemen are also well represented by immigrants in Detroit.

Following a familiar pattern of Arab immigration, many who settled in Detroit, particularly Lebanese and Palestinians, encouraged family members and other relatives to join them. Friends of the immigrating families frequently followed their example. In this way entire extended families and village networks were transferred from Middle Eastern countries to this great American industrial city.

"Detroit is the Arabs' Ellis Island today." Several Arab Americans we met in Detroit made this comparison between Detroit and Ellis Island, the famous immigrant

The bakery of Saleh Houmaye in Dearborn specializes in Arab breads and pastries. He is Lebanese.

A Lebanese Muslim wedding reception in Dearborn. Traditional Arab musical instruments are played while the bride and groom have the first dance.

processing center in Upper New York Bay that opened in 1892 and closed in 1954. Between those years, millions of immigrants sailed past the Statue of Liberty and entered America through Ellis Island.

Today most immigrants to the United States—except Mexicans—arrive at the country's great international airports in Boston, Chicago, Houston, Los Angeles, New York, and many other cities. For Arab immigrants arriving in the U.S., Detroit is the number-one port of entry. In recent years, three out of every five immigrants to greater Detroit have been Arabs, making Arab Americans Detroit's fastest growing ethnic minority.

* * *

Not a street scene in the Middle East but a block in Dearborn's Dix sections where many of the area's Arab immigrants come to do their daily business.

Religious and business symbols are found side by side in Dearborn's heavily Arab Dix section.

This dramatic mural showing Arab immigrants in their new home as well as in the home they left appears on a wall in Dearborn's Dix section.

The Americanization of these boys from Yemen is almost complete, it would seem, as they play football in a Dearborn street. In the background are the smokestacks of the Ford River Rouge assembly plant, where many Arab immigrants have found employment.

The American Muslim Society in Dearborn has a weekend school in the basement of a mosque. The school's 350 students—95 percent are from Yemen—study Arabic and the Koran.

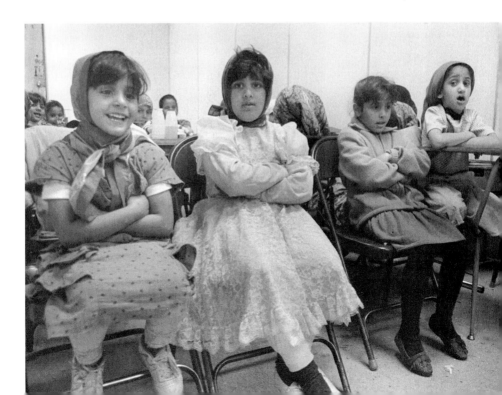

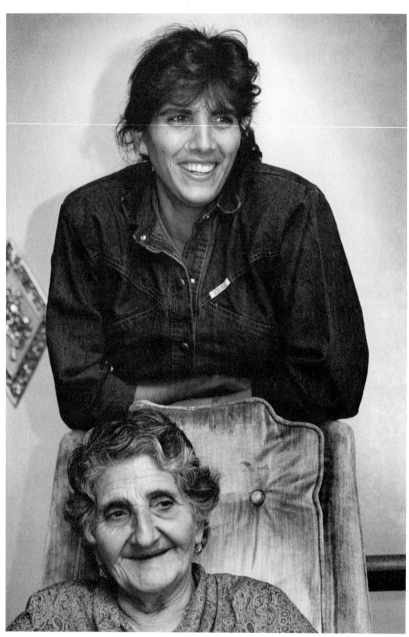

Terry Ahwal and her grandmother, Farideh Abu Martha.

50

Detroit was Terry Ahwal's Ellis Island. She and her sister Ghada came to the United States in 1972 from the West Bank town of Ramallah and lived in Detroit with an aunt and uncle who had been there for several years. Terry was fifteen, her sister seventeen. "After the 1967 war, there was a lot of tension in Ramallah," Terry told us, "confrontations between Palestinian students and Israeli soldiers and sometimes violence. My parents were afraid we'd get involved, so they sent us to Detroit. Since then my mother and father and eight other members of my family have followed us here. We are part of the many Ramallans who have immigrated to the United States."

Paul and I were aware of that remarkable exodus. Ramallah is only a few miles from Jerusalem and is inevitably caught up in much of the tension that blankets that city. Persons who have left Ramallah to live in the United States since the creation of Israel number in the thousands. A Ramallah Federation, with chapters in most large cities, has been formed in America. Every year the Ramallah Federation holds a reunion convention in some U.S. city. Three to five thousand Ramallans from every part of the country attend.

Terry's full name is Taghrid Terese Ahwal. Taghrid, a lovely Arabic name that means "the singing of birds," was the name she had grown up with in Ramallah. "But when I got to Detroit," Terry said, "my uncle said, 'The first thing you have to do is change your name.' He told me that no one would be able to understand or pronounce Taghrid. So I became Terry.

"I came to Detroit at a very sensitive age. At home I was a popular kid. I was involved in everything—drama, athletics, everything you could think of. I was a student in a private school with just sixteen in my class. Here in Detroit the system was completely different, and there were seven hundred in my class. Nobody went out of their way to help me and make me feel comfortable. I was just a faceless part of the crowd, and I wasn't used to that."

Terry graduated from high school and began taking courses in public administration at the University of Michigan at Dearborn; her goal was to complete prelaw requirements and then enter law school. But she had to earn money to go to college, so after high school she worked as a doughnut seller, a waitress, a cashier, a secretary.

She didn't mind the hard work. "We believe in the work ethic," Terry said, speaking of Palestinians. "We are taught to be productive. That is drilled into us from the time we can understand."

Terry became interested in community service and joined the Dearborn police force as a reserve officer. She liked some of the work, especially police programs of activities for young people. But after a few months she resigned as a police reserve officer.

"I couldn't get used to carrying a gun," she said. "I lived through the '67 war. I remember the guns. I can't stand the sound of thunder to this day."

Terry learned soon enough that the large Arab-American population in Detroit made that ethnic group an easy target for prejudice and discrimination. Events in the Middle East since the early 1970s—terrorist activities, an oil embargo by Arab countries, the rise in oil prices—have brought on attacks on Arab Americans in the Detroit area. While the attacks are relatively few, they are very real: the stoning of Arab-American school students whenever a Middle East hostage crisis makes newspaper headlines; bomb threats against Arab-American restaurant owners; the vandalizing of Arab-American businesses and an Arab-American home in a neighborhood where they were the only non-Anglo family.

"Some people's minds are made up that we are terrorists or trouble makers," Terry said. "They don't realize that many of us came here to escape violence and hatred. We aren't about to bring that kind of thing with us. I've had people say to me, 'You don't seem like an Arab.' I'm sure they thought they were saying something nice to me."

For the past two years Terry has been the Detroit representative of the Arab-American Anti-Discrimination Committee. In that job she finds legal help for Arab Americans who are having discrimination problems, and she works with the media in presenting a better Arab-American image to the community.

"I'm still interested in community service," Terry said. "Fighting discrimination is a contribution to the community."

Problems of discrimination and image became even more serious for Arab Americans when Iraq invaded Kuwait, its oil-rich neighbor, on August 2, 1990. Large numbers of American troops were sent to Saudi Arabia to guard that country against possible Iraqi attack and to protect American oil interests.

Almost all major Arab-American organizations publicly condemned Iraq's actions. Nevertheless, the Arab-American Anti-Discrimination Committee reported a nationwide wave of anti-Arab sentiment that brought death threats and physical injury to scores of Arab Americans. The Committee called for FBI help in safeguarding Arab Americans throughout the country.

Arab-American leaders pointed out that many Arab Americans were serving in the United States armed forces in the Persian Gulf and Saudi Arabia. These spokesmen also stressed that the last thing Arab Americans want is a war in the Middle East where they all have family and friends.

Ahmad Suleiman in the laboratory at New Orleans University.

Osama Siblani is publisher of *Sada al-Watan*, a Detroit newspaper for Arab Americans. "For Arab Americans, this is their first country," Mr. Siblani told *The New York Times*. "America is where they chose to live. They fled persecution, oppression, and poverty. And now they will try to prevent a catastrophe on both ends."

Ahmad Suleiman, like Terry Ahwal, is in many ways representative of recent Arab immigrants from the Middle East. Today Ahmad lives with his wife and two children in New Orleans, where he works for a chemical company and teaches a graduate course in chemistry at New Orleans University; but he was born in the Palestinian town of Tulkarm, which is about forty miles from Jerusalem, in 1943.

"Actually," Ahmad told Paul and me when we talked

55

to him in his university office, "my family lived in Alras, a village on the outskirts of Tulkarm. My father was a farmer, and we had sixty hectares of land scattered around Alras in small pieces. It was a case of this olive tree being ours and that one belonging to a neighbor. Everybody knew to whom the trees belonged. All our land was within a half hour's walk of town. Our family income came from olives, wheat, and vegetables."

Ahmad's earliest memory comes from the time in 1948 when Israel proclaimed itself a nation. Tulkarm was just outside the boundary of the newly formed country. "My father told me that we could no longer visit friends in a nearby village because the Jews had taken it. One of my uncles lived in that village, and he had to move into a camp without water, where he was totally dependent on others to stay alive. I couldn't understand how that could be. He had always led a good and dignified life, just as we had."

In the fighting that took place between the Arab countries and Israel in 1948, Jordan annexed a part of Palestine west of the Jordan River that is known today as the West Bank. The town of Tulkarm is in this area, and Ahmad remembers that life for his family was relatively quiet between 1948 and 1967. He went to high school and then graduated with a diploma from an agricultural college in Tulkarm.

Then, in 1967, in what is now known as the Six-Day

War, the Israeli army inflicted a humiliating defeat on the armies of Egypt, Syria, and Jordan. The Israeli army captured the Old City of Jerusalem and occupied all of the West Bank, an occupation that continues to this day.

"Our family was shattered," Ahmad told us. "I have five brothers and sisters. Some were working in east Jordan and were not allowed to return to the West Bank after Israeli occupation. By pure chance, I had taken a teaching job in Saudi Arabia—teaching math and science to elementary-school children—and the Israelis would not allow me to return to my home in Tulkarm except as a visitor. Since that time I have visited home only twice, in 1971 and 1985, for a total of three weeks. Of course I was happy to see the land again, but it was sad to go as a tourist to the house in which I was born.

"The Israeli army has confiscated much of the land. To be told that your home is no longer yours is something that I will never understand or accept. When my mother was dying, I could not go to see her. Getting permission from the military authorities was impossible. One of the things that made me saddest on my last visit was to see that most of the land around Tulkarm is uncultivated. I have childhood memories of people working happily in the fields and of their celebrating when the harvest was finished."

Rather than stay marooned in Saudi Arabia, Ahmad Suleiman decided to come to the United States to go to college, and he was successful in his application for a student visa. "I had always wanted to get a college degree," he said. "Education has always been a priority for Palestinians. My father, a farmer, insisted that we had to get a degree. Even in refugee camps where people live in poverty, a family's primary goal is to send their first son to a university."

We asked Ahmad why he had chosen the United States as a place to study.

"I knew the U.S. was the only place I could go and support myself while I went to college," he said. "I had to have a job. There was no one who could send me money. I had to make my own way."

Because he had a Palestinian friend studying there, Ahmad applied to Texas A&M University and was accepted. His flight to the United States landed in Houston, and Ahmad caught a bus to the hotel where he was to stay overnight before going on to Texas A&M at College Station.

"Destiny plays such an important role in our lives," Ahmad told us. "Can you imagine? The driver of the bus was an Arab, and he knew I was. He spoke to me in Arabic. I was overjoyed because my English was still very poor. The driver convinced me that Houston would be an easier place to find a job and support myself."

Ahmad enrolled at Texas A&M but transferred to the University of Houston as soon as he could. He received his Bachelor of Science degree in chemistry in 1975. "Getting that degree was hard because I had to work the graveyard shift at a supermarket, from eleven at night to seven in the morning. Some days I had early classes, so I just washed my face, grabbed my books, and went to class. Later I was able to change from the graveyard shift, but I kept on working from three in the afternoon until eleven at night until I got my Master of Science degree in 1978."

That same year he moved to New Orleans when the University of New Orleans offered him a teaching assistantship. After moving, he married a Palestinian woman, Mai, whom he had met in Houston. She had arrived there as an immigrant in 1974. Ahmad and Mai became U.S. citizens in 1986. They have two sons, ages six and one.

Paul asked Ahmad if they intend to teach their children Arabic. "We want them to speak and understand Arabic as well as English," Ahmad said. "We are Muslims, and Arabic is the language of our religion. With the older boy we emphasize that he is originally Palestinian so that he won't forget his heritage. As much as we can, we take part in Arab-American activities in New Orleans, such as weddings. When we go to an event where people wear traditional clothing, we tell our son that this is the way your aunts and uncles dress. There are about two thousand Arab Americans in New Or-

Karim and Sajida Khudairi live in the Boston suburb of Wellesley; both are retired biologists who have taught at the university level. Mr. Khudairi is presently president of the Islamic Center in nearby Quincy. Originally from Iraq, the Khudairis moved back to that country at one point so that their children could learn Arabic. "It was very important to us," Mr. Khudairi said. "Their first language was English, and it was not enough to hear their parents speaking Arabic. We realized that to learn Arabic they would have to live in a country where it is spoken."

leans, I think. We do not have a mosque yet, but one is planned."

Speaking of Arab Americans, Ahmad said, "It is essential that we participate fully in the mainstream life of this country. It is true that we have little experience with democracy—it didn't exist in the Middle East— but we have a beautiful culture and much to contribute to the United States. We have to overcome the stereo-

60

typing. In this country the word Palestinian has such bad connotations. It conjures up pictures of terrorists, hijacking, the murder of innocent people. But we are human beings just like you. At home we lived like an average middle-class American family."

In the process of becoming Americanized, Ahmad has become a great football fan. "My wife doesn't like me during football season," he said, "but even she has gotten so that she will watch an occasional game with me. My favorite team is the Dallas Cowboys. Of course I arrived in Texas knowing only soccer. I had no idea what football was. The first game I went to was between the University of Houston and the University of Tennessee at the Astrodome. I went with a friend, and I kept saying, 'Where is the ball?' I couldn't see it. I couldn't understand the game very well. And baseball—I've just bought my son a bat and am teaching him how to hit the ball."

Ahmad drove us to the airport, and again he talked about his original home. "I am glad that I came to the United States," he said. "There is opportunity here if you want to work. But the attachment to my home where I grew up is still there. It is a place so dear to my heart, and I do not think that is bad. In the spring the mountains will be covered with olive trees and almond trees in bloom. It is very beautiful. I dream of them, and so does my wife."

FIVE

"I Have This Longing"

Ahmad Suleiman's sensitive recall of a home, of family and friends, of a beautiful land all lost forever, was a theme that we heard many times in talking with Arab Americans who have come to the United States from Lebanon and Palestine since the beginning of turmoil in those places. In Atlanta we met Dr. Abdallah E. Najjar, who had recently retired from a career of working for the U.S. government, first with the foreign aid program in the fields of malariology and parasitology and later with the U.S. Centers for Disease Control as director of its Office of International Health.

Dr. Najjar's father, we learned, had been born in the

Mount Lebanon village of Baakline about a hundred years ago, in 1887, into a family that practiced the Druze faith. Dr. Najjar's grandfather was the village baker. In those days families would prepare their own dough and then give it to a baker's helper, who would take it to the oven; later he would deliver the freshly baked bread. The job of baker's helper fell to Dr. Najjar's father, who soon realized that this was not the life he wanted. One of his brothers had gone to America the year before. In conversations with people on his bread delivery route, he learned more about the place called the United States, and his imagination was inflamed. In those days, when the Turkish Ottoman Empire was in flux, people kept their wealth stashed away in their homes in gold

Dr. Abdallah Najjar and his wife, Jean, in their backyard garden.

coins. One day Dr. Najjar's father took three gold coins from the family treasure and left a note that said, "I am only borrowing this money. I will pay it back later with interest." With the gold he bought passage on a ship to America. The year was 1903; Dr. Najjar's father was sixteen years old, and he had a third-grade education.

In New York City he found a job cleaning the windows of skyscrapers that were already beginning to dot Manhattan's skyline. Soon he had saved enough money to travel to Spokane, Washington, where his brother was working as a peddler, selling household items to rural communities. By 1907 the two brothers had saved enough money to open a grocery store in Spokane. Dr. Najjar has an old photograph of the store; he also has his father's U.S. citizenship papers, dated 1913.

During World War I, Dr. Najjar's father fought with the U.S. infantry forces in France. In 1920 he returned to Lebanon where he met and married Dr. Najjar's mother—an arranged marriage. Dr. Najjar's father returned to America again in 1926, leaving his family in Lebanon. This time he went to Mullens, West Virginia, because he knew that many Lebanese Americans were working in coal-mining and railroad activities there. He worked first as a peddler around Mullens and then opened a drygoods store there. He visited his family in

Lebanon from time to time and in 1938 returned there to live out his life.

Dr. Najjar was born in Lebanon, in the village of Baakline, but from the moment of his birth, he was an American citizen because his father was an American citizen. He spent the first years of his life in Baakline and went to school there. Later he went to the American University of Beirut for three years, the first member of his immediate family to go to college.

"My father could not educate all his children," Dr. Najjar said. "Only one, and I was fortunate to be the one selected. Since I was the best educated, the others have regarded me as the family's elder statesman."

With outbreak of World War II, Dr. Najjar and his brothers—also U.S. citizens—received their draft notices through the American consulate in Beirut. Dr. Najjar was twenty. He could have chosen to remain in Lebanon and would never have had to fight in the war; but he was proud of his U.S. citizenship, even though he had never been to America. He reported to the American consulate for induction and was sent to an army base in Florida for his basic training. Later, en route to France, his troop ship was hit by a German torpedo but did not sink. Dr. Najjar served eighteen months in France and Germany with the U.S. Army's Third Infantry Division. One of his brothers was sent to the

Pacific and served on Okinawa; another served in the Persian Gulf.

After the war, Dr. Najjar chose West Virginia as his place to be discharged from the army. He had never been there, but he wanted to see the state where his father had spent many of his years in America. "My first reaction was 'How did my father ever wind up here in the sticks?' " Dr. Najjar told us. "Then I realized that he must have been attracted by the mountains. There is a lot of similarity to Lebanon."

Dr. Najjar settled in Mullens, the town where his father had lived. With a brother and a cousin who had also come to the West Virginia town, Dr. Najjar bought a shop that sold ice cream and sandwiches. He used an old '41 Plymouth and three hundred dollars he had saved from his army service as his share of the down payment.

"My main interest was in getting my brother started in business," Dr. Najjar said. "I didn't want him to be working for anybody else. We value our independence and dislike regimentation."

A second brother and two more cousins arrived in Mullens, and Dr. Najjar helped them set up another business, the American Cafe. "Then I went back to college," Dr. Najjar said, "Concord College in Athens, West Virginia. My wife is from West Virginia. We met in college and were married a year and a half after we graduated.

"During all these early years in America," Dr. Najjar continued, "I found myself comparing the new and the old, sorting out values, deciding which values should be kept, which discarded. I am the product of two cultures, of course. This I have always told my sons."

I asked Dr. Najjar to talk about the values of the two cultures of which he is a product. "From the Lebanese culture," he said, "the love of kinfolks, the concern for the extended family. And family honor: I have always told my sons, 'If you dishonor your name, you put a blemish on the whole Najjar name.' Other values from my Lebanese heritage are surely a belief in the work ethic and a belief in the great value of education.

"On the American side: the goodness of the American heart, a humanity that goes beyond the extended family. Americans can and do show their concern for people starving in Ethiopia and people suffering from earthquakes in Peru or Mexico. Straightforwardness: Americans tell it like it is, and that is a good quality. Pragmatism: being practical, finding ways to get things done."

After Concord College, Dr. Najjar went to the School of Public Health at the University of North Carolina, earning a Master's degree in public health. In 1951 he went to work for the U.S. government's foreign-aid program; for the next thirteen years he served in Iran, Ethiopia, Egypt, and Jamaica, earning his Ph.D. along the way. In 1964 he joined the U.S. Centers for Disease Control in Atlanta and worked there until he recently retired.

In the forty-five years since Dr. Najjar left his village in Lebanon, he has returned for visits many times. "I own a little piece of land," he said. "There is not much there, just some grapevines and a few olive trees. And a dug well. The land has been in the family for five hundred years. It came to me through my maternal grandfather. I wanted that piece of land, and my father willed it to me. I didn't want any other part of his estate, which was quite large.

"In 1981 I took one of my sons with me on a trip to the Middle East, and we visited Lebanon. We went to see my little piece of land. It was sundown, a beautiful, lovely winter evening. We could see the sea, a breathtaking sight for him. Even I had forgotten how beautiful it could be. I scooped up a handful of the earth and I said, chokingly, 'Son, this is holy soil.'

"Later, my son said to me, 'Dad, you could have given me a million dollars and it wouldn't have meant as much to me as this visit.' I have always hoped that my sons would feel the same way about the land, even though their attachment might be a little less. We have three sons. They all speak some Arabic. Each of them has spent a summer in a village in Lebanon. They have met their extended family there and have experienced their love and generosity."

And then Dr. Najjar added, "The land has a strong mystique for us Druze. Our family ties are so strong. One feels a sense of guilt for leaving land and family. There is a strong pull in me to go home and die as my father did. I have been in America for forty-five years. Here I am married to an American girl. I am a veteran of World War II. I have worked many years for the United States government. Still, I feel a pull to go home. God has provided for me bountifully in America, but my cultural heritage is strong. I may never go back to live, but I have this longing to go back."

Dr. Najjar is deeply committed to creating a better understanding of Arab Americans in the United States. "I retired early so that I could devote all my time and energy to that cause," he said. "I am the product of a beautiful culture. As an intelligent, educated, well-traveled man, I know there are superior things in my heritage that I can pass along to my children. To succeed in that, I must help stop the defamation that we Arabs are subjected to in movies, the press, television. Our time has come. Other people—Jews, blacks, Hispanics—have gone through this."

Dr. Najjar is vigorously involved in the activities of the approximately ten thousand Arab Americans in the

Atlanta area. He writes for a number of publications on Arab-American matters. He organized and served for years on the Council of Elders of the American Druze Society, a national organization concerned with supporting and creating a better understanding of the Druze faith and theology.

Before we left, Dr. Najjar took us to the small, carefully cultivated garden at the back of their house. "I am not a farmer," he said with a smile, "but when you visit an Arab's home, you will find a grapevine and a fig tree. They are expressions—they are symbolic—of his love of the land."

We admired the grapevine and the fig tree growing in the Najjar garden.

Lamees Al-ayubi, a Palestinian friend of Paul's, first told us about Nahida Fadle Dajani. "I was living in Beirut then," Lamees recalled. "Nahida had a radio program there. It was called, literally translated, 'With the Morning.' She read poetry, sometimes her own, but usually the poetry of other nations that she translated into Arabic. My father would listen to her program every morning, so her voice was always in the background as I was getting ready for school. Even the driver of our school bus would listen. It was a fifteen-minute program that preceded the first newscast of the day.

"I think there are few Arabs, of my generation at least,

Nahida Fadle Dajani

who are not familiar with Nahida's voice. It is a voice that goes right to your heart. At the end of the day she would have another program just before sign-off. I was always in bed by then, but sometimes I heard her. Her voice would give you goose bumps."

We went to see Nahida Dajani in her home in Annandale, Virginia, a Washington, D.C., suburb. She is an animated woman with graceful hands, brown eyes, brown hair. Her manner is friendly and informal. "I love wearing jeans, T-shirts, tennis shoes," she said. "Deep down inside me there is a hippie, I think. It distresses my mother when she sees me."

Nahida came to the United States to live in 1984, following her five children, who—one by one—had immigrated to this country. A member of a large Palestinian family, she was born and raised in Jerusalem and lived there until she was fifteen.

"I remember the colors of Jerusalem," she told us. "They can't be found anyplace else. It was there that I started to write poetry. All adolescents in the Arab world write poetry. My mother was tolerant: I could write about love even then." She changed the subject abruptly. "In 1948 we were put on a truck and sent to Beirut. All our possessions were lost."

Nahida developed her radio program while she was a student at the American University of Beirut. As it took hold and became popular, her program—and her voice—was heard from Lebanon, across Saudi Arabia, and throughout the Persian Gulf states. She was in a way a pioneer, since she was the first woman to be heard on Kuwaiti radio.

Speaking of her poetry, Nahida said, "Love is its central theme: love of the land, love of Jerusalem, love of our people."

Speaking of Arabs and poetry, she said, "We Arabs love poetry. We are all poets. We live by it. We don't have classical music. We have poetry. It is our heritage."

Nahida's life has been one of moving from one country to another. She lived fifteen years in Jerusalem, thirty in Lebanon, and one in Cyprus before moving to Washington. Like most Palestinian families, Nahida's has been scattered. She has brothers living in California, Maryland, and London; sisters in Kuwait and Jordan. Her mother lives in Jordan but sometimes visits her in Washington.

"It is the lot of the modern Palestinian to be scattered," she said. "For two years after my arrival here, I lived in isolation. I spent all my time writing angry letters to Beirut saying, 'I don't deserve this. Nobody knows me. I'm just a number here.' At home it was difficult for me to walk down the street without being recognized; here I was nobody. And then one day I simply took myself in hand and said, 'You can't spend the rest of your life wallowing in self-pity.' I changed just like that. Now I feel privileged to live in such a culturally beautiful city as Washington.

"Here I don't feel alienated. I am a comfortable part of this mixture of immigrants. But if you ask me where I really belong, I will say Jerusalem. We didn't have the choice of leaving. Or of returning. Even the name of our country has been changed. In a perfect world everyone in my family would live within easy walking distance of each other in Jerusalem."

At a recent poetry recital in Washington, Nahida began her presentation with this introduction: "Once in my life I was in Jerusalem. Now she is in me, and she will always be my first love. Once in my life I was in Beirut. Now she is in me, and she will always be my second love. Washington is a question. Is there a place for more love in my heart? I know the answer is yes."

Nahida still tapes a weekly thirty-minute radio program that is broadcast throughout the Middle East. "Even though I cannot go back to Jerusalem, my voice can return," she said. "I can live with my people through my voice. Now and then I meet Palestinians who have chosen to remain in Israel, and they tell me that they know me and that they feel we are friends. I sometimes cry when they say, 'You are one of us. You didn't leave.'"

One subject came up often when we talked to Arab Americans, especially Palestinians and Lebanese who felt that Israel was largely or entirely responsible for the dislocation in their lives. The subject was how they felt about or what they thought about American Jews and the almost total support that the American Jewish population gives to Israel. Most felt that this support, and particularly the activities of the American Israel Public Affairs Committee, a powerful American Jewish pro-Israel lobbying organization in Washington, D.C., had the effect of turning American public opinion against Arabs, including Arab Americans.

Dr. Nabeel Abraham, an Arab American, is a research associate at Wayne State University's Center for Urban Studies in Detroit. "Arab Americans bear the burden of the Israeli-Arab conflict," he told us. "It is an issue constantly alive. Arabs feel a sense of alienation. The plight of Arabs is never discussed in this country. We have a difficult time getting into the debate when we have something to say. The American people are always concerned about the problems of others. Why, we say, can't they be concerned about ours? This alienates us. We feel unwelcome. We have a feeling of justice denied."

Terry Ahwal explained her feelings this way: "If anybody has a reason to be prejudiced against Jews it is me. I saw my father beaten by Jews in Israel, and I lived under their occupation for five years. But I try not to generalize about Jews. There are so many kinds. There are those who are against any and all Arabs, just in general; in their eyes, we are all Israel's enemy. But there are lots of Jews who come and work within the Arab community; some of them are more outspoken than Arabs about Israeli occupation of the West Bank and the Israeli invasion of Lebanon in 1982. Then there are Jews who don't participate in the debate at all."

Frank and Lena Afranji are Palestinians who immigrated to the United States at different times and married in this country. They live in Portland, Oregon, where he is an analyst for Portland General Electric and she is a first-year optometry student at Pacific University. Frank is very much aware of the support that American Jews give to Israel. "We must copy the Jewish

Frank and Lena Afranji

experience," he told us. "Wherever a Jew might be, his focus is on Israel. They worked and still work to support Israel. Palestinians have to do the same to achieve a Palestinian homeland. Every Palestinian, wherever he is—in some little country in Central America or in China—has to do something."

Because they fear Jewish voter disapproval, American politicians are reluctant to seek or even accept Arab-American support. Norman Assed, a very warm and friendly Arab-American businessman we met in Albuquerque, New Mexico, told us of his experience involving politics. He attended a fund-raiser in Albuquerque for Michael Dukakis, the Democratic

Party presidential candidate in the 1988 election. At the event Norman met Dukakis' father-in-law.

"Later in the evening," Norman told us, "I saw someone across the room pointing at me while he was talking to Dukakis' father-in-law. Afterward I learned that he was saying, 'Whatever you do, don't be seen with that guy. He's a Palestinian. Be sure you're not photographed with him.' I really was shocked."

This kind of political reaction to Arab Americans is by no means unusual. In 1988, James Abourezk, an Arab American and former United States senator, sent a one-hundred-dollar campaign contribution to Joseph P. Kennedy II, who was running for Congress in Massa-

Norman Assed. Photo by David Conklin.

chusetts' 8th District. The contribution was returned to Abourezk by one of Kennedy's aides. According to *The Washington Post*, the aide felt the contribution might be too controversial since Abourezk is chairman of the Arab-American Anti-Discrimination Committee, which takes a sympathetic view of the Palestine Liberation Organization.

In a letter to Joe Kennedy, Abourezk wrote, "I think you know that I ran, and won, as a delegate for your father, the late senator Robert F. Kennedy, in 1968. I have supported your uncles each time they have sought national office, primarily because of their courage—and that of your father's—in facing tough and controversial issues."

Later, Joe Kennedy apologized for the return of Abourezk's contribution and said that if it were resubmitted, "I'd be quite honored to accept."

In a 1988 article in *The Washington Post*, James Zogby, director of the Arab American Institute, wrote: "For years Arab Americans have worked to no avail to meet with national party leadership and be recognized as a constituent group. Our community still remembers the pain when the Mondale campaign returned contributions made by Arab-American Democrats in 1984."

Over one hundred thousand Arab Americans live in New York City, many of them merchants and restaurant owners located along Atlantic Avenue in Brooklyn.

During the 1989 election campaigns for mayor of New York, there were many complaints from Arab-American groups that both Democratic candidate David N. Dinkins and Republican candidate Rudolph W. Giuliani refused to meet with them or to accept their offers of support. Arab-American leaders in New York said that both the Democratic and Republican campaign managers were concerned that accepting Arab-American help, either financial or as campaign volunteer workers, would bring about an adverse reaction among New York's Jewish voters.

But all is not dark in terms of relations between Arab Americans and Jewish Americans. In a number of U.S. cities with large Arab-American and Jewish populations, some members of both ethnic groups are striving for better relations and increasing understanding of each other. Washington, D.C., is one of those places. For some time now Arab Americans and Jews in the Washington area have been coming together for "friendship" dinners, to get better acquainted and to explore issues that divide them. Those issues as defined by one of the organizations, Washington Area Jews for Israeli-Palestinian Peace, are the occupation by Israel of Palestinian lands, the statelessness of the Palestinians, and the failure of most of the Arab world to recognize Israel and its right to exist.

About the friendship dinners, Ellen Siegel, one of the

Mary Lahaj, a delegate from South Weymouth, Massachusetts, to the 1988 National Democratic Convention. Her grandparents came to the United States from Lebanon at the turn of the century. She was one of fifty-five Arab-American delegates to the 1988 convention; in 1984 there were only four.

80

founding members of Washington Area New Jewish Agenda, said, "I wanted Jews to meet Palestinians because the word Palestinian had become so stereotyped. Many Jews had never met one. I also wanted Palestinians to know that there were Jews who were concerned about the plight of Palestinians."

Los Angeles has large Arab-American and Jewish communities. In the last few years at least half a dozen "dialogue" groups made up of Arab Americans and Jews—groups with such names as the Middle East Cousins Club of America—have been formed to discuss problems between Arabs and Jews in the Middle East and to explore the ways by which they might be solved.

Recently the groups came together in the garden of the Los Angeles city hall for the planting of two olive trees that would symbolize their hopes for peace and understanding between Arabs and Jews. Casey Kasem, one of the speakers at the ceremony, put those hopes into words when he said, "Side by side we plant these trees, and side by side our peoples will flourish."

S I X

Work

The story of immigrants whose hard work brings success in America is a familiar one. Perhaps no particular immigrant nationality exceeds others in the capacity for work; nevertheless, Paul and I were struck by the willingness of every Arab-American immigrant we talked with to toil long hours, often at several jobs at the same time, to attain an education, buy a store, accumulate money to bring other family members to America, and—most of all—to achieve a place in America.

"We believe in the work ethic," Terry Ahwal had said to us, and she introduced us to her uncle, Joe Martha, as a prime example of what she was talking about.

The Martha family lives in Monroe, a town near Detroit. Joe and his wife Rozette own a convenience store ("party store") and in the best mom-and-pop tradition are the entire staff. They have four children who range in age from eleven to eighteen, and Joe's mother lives with them. The night we visited the Marthas, Rozette went to the store to relieve Joe so that he could come and talk with us. He came to Detroit from Ramallah in 1965, we learned, following two brothers who had received rare visas to come in 1956 and 1959. There was no fortune in Ramallah, Joe had concluded, so he decided to seek one in America.

Joe Martha serving dinner for his family and Terry Ahwal.

"I will never forget the country I came from," Joe said, "and I will never forget the opportunity I found in this country, which is now my country."

Joe knew how to take advantage of the work opportunities that were in his new country. "I'm a hustler," Joe said to us. "When I first came here, I worked three jobs at a time. Every morning I had to take four buses to get to work. I saved my money and after the '67 war I brought my parents, three sisters, and a nephew. Later I brought Terry and her sister and half a dozen other members of the family. Altogether I brought over sixteen. That left me with five hundred dollars. I borrowed some money in 1969 and started a party store."

Joe talked again about being a Palestinian. "Ramallah and Palestine are still very close to me. I always say that I am a Palestinian American. My mother loves America because her family lives here safely, but she loves Palestine because that is where Jesus was born. We don't want our kids to forget their heritage. English is their language, but we speak to them in Arabic also so they won't forget their roots. And of course we Americanize. My oldest son's name is Shuchry, but we call him Chuck."

I asked Joe if the family or anyone in it had experienced anti-Arab discrimination.

"Not much," he said, "but sometimes something ugly

Joe Martha's mother, Farideh Abu Martha. "My mother loves America because her family lives safely here," Joe says. "She loves Palestine because that is where Jesus was born."

happens. Chuck had his jaw broken in a fight when he was called a camel jockey."

Chuck—who was not at home on the night of our visit—is sixteen, and the broken jaw ended a promising football career. Neither was Dena, the oldest of the Martha children, present that night; she is eighteen and can legally work in the party store, which sells beer and wine. She was at work. But we met thirteen-year-old Zezette (she is called Tootsie) and Charlie, who is eleven. Charlie's room was filled with baseball and other sports equipment, and Tootsie had a big poster of rock star George Michael displayed on a wall of her room. Tootsie has already decided that she wants to be a lawyer. Charlie hasn't made up his mind.

Talking later about his children, Joe said, "For twenty years I have worked sixteen hours a day, seven days a week. Day and night I talk to my kids telling them they have to go to college so they won't have to work this hard."

And then Joe said (a bit wistfully, I thought), "I would love to go to college, too, but who's going to feed them if I do? When they start to college, I will have to work even harder."

Halim Awde and his family live in a lovely house in Dedham, Massachusetts, a suburb of Boston. Halim owns a filling station in nearby Quincy, and running it keeps him busy day and night. Still, he finds time to serve as liaison to the Boston mayor's office for the Arab-American community in the area. Halim and his wife, Lebebe, are originally from Lebanon. They invited Paul and me to their house for dinner one night, and Lebebe prepared a dazzling array of Lebanese food, including such boyhood favorites of mine as *kibbeh*, stuffed vine leaves, chicken with rice and tomatoes, and a won-

Halim and Lebebe Awde with their children.

derful salad called *fattoush*. Of course, there were some great Lebanese desserts.

"There is one thing about my culture," Halim said. "We feed a guest until he can't eat any more, and then we expect him to eat some more. If you don't eat in my house, you don't like me."

From the amount I ate that night, I must qualify as one of Halim's best friends.

During dinner Halim talked about Arab stereotypes. "Most Americans think that all Arabs live in the desert and ride camels," he said. "They get that idea from movies and cartoons. The first camel I saw was in the Cleveland zoo, and I've never seen a desert except in a movie.

"And Arabs aren't supposed to care about anything but making money and buying big cars. People never hear about how much we love poetry—more than any other people, I think. I write poetry. I teach my kids to rhyme in both Arabic and English. At the University of Houston one of my teachers told me that she could tell which papers had been written by Lebanese students just by the romantic way we described nature and the way we talked about the mountains, the sea, and the places where we lived.

"But it's true," Halim continued, "that Lebanese are the most ambitious people on earth. At least, that's what I think. We value education, but I know multimillion-aires who don't know how to read and write. And Lebanese go everywhere. There was a cartoon in a Beirut newspaper once. It showed Lebanese greeting the astronauts when they landed on the moon. My grandfather went to Cuba after World War II. My mother is Lebanese, but she was born in Cuba; later she went to Lebanon to live, but she is still fluent in Spanish. I have cousins in Ohio who speak Spanish at home."

Later Halim talked about work. "I really learned to work in America," he said. "This country made a man of me. The U.S. was built on the work ethic. What made this country great was hard work. My kids are going to learn to work. My oldest daughter already mows the lawn. As soon as my son George is twelve, he will start helping me at the station."

Halim told us how he got started in America, a story that was becoming a familiar one to us. He came to the U.S. in 1970 to go to college and enrolled in business administration at the University of Houston.

"To pay my way in school I worked at Jack-in-the-Box, Kentucky Fried Chicken, and filling stations, always at least eight hours a day while I was going to school full-time. I lied to my parents. I didn't want them to know what kind of jobs I was doing, and what I was going through. If he had known the truth, my father would have taken the next plane and brought me back home to Lebanon. So I told them I had an office job paying twelve dollars an hour.

"One summer I needed $150 to register for summer school. I had no money. At home it is shameful to borrow, but I was desperate. I called an uncle in Cleveland, who had been there for thirty years. He sent me a check and a letter which said, 'Please send the money back soon because I have to feed my family.' I felt like a beggar. I was so upset that I sent the money back the next day. And then—it is almost impossible to believe—I won a lottery for exactly $150. The good Lord provides."

The civil war that has consumed Lebanon since the seventies brought about a decision on Halim's part—and on his family's part—that he should remain in the United States. The decision was reinforced by the death of one of Halim's older brothers from a sniper's bullet.

Lebebe and Halim had known each other from childhood in their village in Lebanon. In 1976 she came to Boston, where members of her family had lived for years, and they were married there. They lived in Houston initially but later moved to Boston. Lebebe's family owns a chain of filling stations in the Boston area; with the money they had saved in Houston, family guidance, and Halim's business administration experience, Halim and Lebebe became filling station owners. In time Halim helped one of his brothers get into the filling station business.

90

"It is hard to get your gas tank filled in Boston without buying from a Lebanese," Lebebe said.

And, I thought, it is hard to find a better example of how family support and a capacity for lots and lots of work result in a satisfying success story.

Merhej Srour is a welder, one of the more than five thousand Arab Americans who work in the automobile manufacturing and assembly plants of Dearborn. In 1974 Merhej came to the United States from the Lebanese village of Shihin, which is in the southern part of Lebanon near the Israeli border. Although that part of the country is tense and strife-ridden—many Palestinian refugees live there—Merhej immigrated to America mainly for economic reasons.

He tried several jobs after his arrival—working in a restaurant and filling station, even selling clothes door-to-door—before he entered a government job-training program and learned the welding trade. In 1976 he went to work as a welder for the Chrysler Corporation. The work was steady, sometimes with overtime, and the pay good enough that he was able to save money for a down payment on a house. He had started a family, and that was important.

And then in 1980 a recession hit the automotive industry, and Merhej was laid off indefinitely. He was called back for a short time and then laid off again. That has continued to be the pattern to this day.

We visited Merhej's home, met his wife and children. The house contains the bare minimum of furnishings, but the children are healthy, and the five who are in school are doing well at their studies. Merhej and his wife speak to them in Arabic at home because they are a Muslim family, and Arabic is important to their religion.

Despite the bleak outlook in the automotive industry, Merhej is not pessimistic about the future. "We live day to day," he said, "but still we know how to save. We do not spend money on foolish things. We know that if we

Merhej Srour and his family.

have a hundred dollars we do not have to spend all of it. If I cannot get enough work in the factories, I will start a little store. We have not yet saved enough for that, but we will. I am not worried. We will be all right."

Kahlil Gibran is an Arab name known and admired by millions of Americans. Born in Lebanon in 1883, Gibran immigrated to the United States with his family in 1894 when he was eleven. Except for a four-year return to Beirut to study, Gibran lived the rest of his relatively short life in Boston and New York. Artist and writer, he produced a huge body of work. His paintings and drawings were compared by the sculptor Auguste Rodin to those of William Blake.

But it was Kahlil Gibran's book *The Prophet*, published in 1923, that made him famous and that has captured the attention and feelings of generations of Americans, particularly young Americans. It is a book, mystical in tone, that deals with love, friendship, joy, sorrow, and all other human feelings and emotions. In *The Prophet* and his other books, his message essentially concerned the brotherhood of man and the supreme healing power of love. More than seven million copies of *The Prophet* have been sold in the United States and over one hundred thousand copies are still sold each year. Kahlil Gibran died in 1931, but his fame endures.

In Boston, Paul and I met another Kahlil Gibran, a

distant relative and godson of his famous namesake. The present Kahlil Gibran is himself an artist, a sculptor of national reputation whose work in bronze, hammered steel, and other materials resides in some of the best fine-arts museums, galleries, and private collections in the country. He has written, "My subject matter is man first and foremost," and one of his inspirations for his sculpture is the Bible. One of his most famous and powerful works in bronze is of John the Baptist. He has sculpted David and three different visions of Job. His *Pietà* received the Gold Medal Award for Excellence at the International Show of Religious Art in Trieste, Italy, in 1966. In 1959 and 1960 he received John Simon Guggenheim awards to advance his work.

Kahlil lives with his wife Jean in a spacious house on a quiet, tree-lined street in South Boston. The Gibran house, as we discovered on our visit, is the focus of an enormous amount of creative energy. Kahlil came down the steps onto the street to meet us. He is a dynamo always on the move, even when he is seated. Like many Lebanese we had met, he punctuates every sentence with hand gestures. His glasses constantly slip down on his nose, and he constantly pushes them back.

He ushered us into the hallway of his house and past a bust of the earlier Kahlil Gibran that he had recently sculpted. The front room of the house serves as a sitting and display room and contains a number of his sculp-

Kahlil Gibran with his bronze bust of his famous godfather, writer/poet/artist Kahlil Gibran.

tures, large and small. We followed him around the house, fascinated. There was no formal beginning to our conversation, no need to ask questions, although I occasionally was able to slip one in. For the most part we just listened.

"I have a lot of energy," he said, stating the obvious. "All I want to do is work." Ten years ago, he told us, he fought off melanoma, a particularly serious form of cancer. "But I didn't let it slow me down. I'm sixty-five. Time is running out for me. I don't leave a minute unused. I touch on everything. I'm like an octopus."

And so he is. Kahlil leaves no creative stone unturned. Consider some of the things he does:

He writes: He and his wife spent two and a half years researching and writing the definitive biography of his illustrious kinsman; it is entitled *Kahlil Gibran: His Life and Work*.

He re-creates old musical instruments.

He restores old paintings and furniture: He has restored more than thirty paintings by Gilbert Stuart, the eighteenth-century American portrait master.

He is an inventor.

He plays pool.

He is an authority on old Chinese coins.

He wins cooking contests.

He has assembled what he believes is the largest private collection of medals in America.

He builds cameras, and designs and builds other photographic equipment.

And all this of course is in addition to the long hours that he puts into his primary work as a sculptor. Every other sentence is punctuated with "Let me show you something." His tangents have tangents as he moves from subject to subject with bewildering speed. "There's no material I can't handle. I weld with steel. I work ivory. I'm not bragging. I just do it."

And he isn't bragging. There is no sense of self-satisfaction or self-congratulation in Kahlil Gibran. There is simply that great need to create.

He took a beautiful cue stick from a padded case and

Kahlil Gibran playing the *vihuela*, a double-stringed lute, predecessor of the Spanish guitar. This vihuela, which was made by Gibran himself, has been played by guitarists Carlos Montoya and Andrés Segovia and by folksinger-guitarist Richie Havens.

showed it to us. "My doctor said to me, 'You have to do something that will take care of stress.' So I decided to take up pool. I went to a local pool parlor and found a Damon Runyon character who talked about 'deeze guys' and 'doze guys.' I paid him sixty dollars a week, and he tutored me for two years. Now every week I go down to a pool hall beneath Fenway Park and beat everybody in sight. I never gamble a dime. The others can't understand that. It's the inner game that fascinates me."

Kahlil never does anything halfway. He wants to master everything he tries. It was only natural that he made his own cue using a new design with the weight shifted in a different way.

"I'm an inventor, too," he said as he brought out an aluminum camera tripod. It looked like a piece of modern sculpture and was in no way a conventional tripod. "Brookstone Company is making two thousand of these and will market them," he added. He showed us a 600mm camera lens that he had made in 1953. Paul was awed. He had never seen such a lens, and he marveled at its compactness.

In another room I saw a beautiful steel pot with a golden squid on the lid. I asked him about the lovely creation. "I'm a terrific cook," he said. "I made the pot for my squid spaghetti that won first prize two years ago."

As we talked further about food, we learned that he

98

is a mycologist, an authority on mushrooms, and knows two hundred varieties by their Latin names.

Later, when we stopped for some tea, I had the chance to ask Kahlil about his memories of his godfather, the first Kahlil Gibran. "My family lived in Boston's Chinatown, and Kahlil Gibran lived next door," he said. "I remember that he used to take a clock apart and give me a prize if I could reassemble it. Once he gave me a five-dollar gold piece. I went to Quincy school. I'd be playing marbles at recess, and Kahlil Gibran would be walking by in his straw hat, carrying a cane. He was very elegant. I sensed somehow that he was important. Sometimes he would take me for a walk and buy me an ice cream ball dipped in chocolate. He always treated me as an equal, like I was an important person."

I asked Kahlil about his beginnings as an artist. "My father was a cabinetmaker and craftsman. I worked with him when I was a boy. All my life I knew I would go to art school and that I would be an artist," he said, "even though I was a whiz in math, physics, and chemistry, too. I could have been a doctor or a scientist, but because of Kahlil Gibran's influence, my parents wanted me to be an artist.

"We were poor when I was a boy. I didn't go to a restaurant until I was eighteen. My father was extremely proud and told me not even to look in restaurants when I passed them. But when I was ready to go to the Boston

Museum School of Fine Arts, my father had just the two hundred dollars that I needed for the first year's fees. I left art school after three years because I was worried about money but mainly because I knew I was ready to begin my work."

When we resumed our roaming of the house, he took us to the basement and showed us his collection of old medals—Renaissance and Napoleonic medallions, presidential peace medals, U.S. historical medals—which he keeps neatly arrayed in a cabinet. He has been collecting them for thirty years and has two thousand.

"Once I was in a Boston junk shop, and I asked if they had any medals," he said. "The owner brought out a tray, and there was an Aldus Manutius. I bought it for twenty-five dollars, and it turned out that there is only one other in existence."

I confessed that I had no idea who Aldus Manutius was. Kahlil looked surprised. "Why," he said, "a fifteenth-century Venetian printer."

But, as I discovered later, there is a practical point to Kahlil's medal collecting. An important segment of his work is the making of small bronze plaques of human figures, including biblical persons. His study of the work of great medallion makers of the past has added to his skill and feeling for the medium.

In one corner of Kahlil's basement workshop were stacks of small metal disks with holes in them. Paul asked him what they were, and Kahlil remarked offhandedly that they were 200-B.C. Chinese coins that he was identifying for a Boston rare-coin dealer.

Kahlil speaks with as pure a Boston accent as I have ever heard, and despite his Lebanese background, it just did not occur to me that he might speak Arabic. But at one point in our visit with Kahlil we were joined by Halim Awde, one of our Boston hosts, and he and Kahlil began speaking in Arabic. When I remarked that I hadn't had any indication that Kahlil spoke Arabic, Halim said, "Oh, he speaks very beautiful Arabic."

I should have known that, of course.

Late in the afternoon, Jean Gibran, Kahlil's wife, returned home from the elementary school where she teaches. She has been a teacher for twenty years, she told me. While Paul was photographing Kahlil, Jean and I talked about him.

"I think he represents creativity in its highest form," she said. "He takes risks and follows through. He has stamina. Every day is a challenge. Every day there is something to discover. He will track down what he is after like a bulldog. He will find everything that is relevant to a subject and study it until he has mastered it."

That, I thought, summed up Kahlil Gibran, godson of another artistic genius named Kahlil Gibran, very well.

SEVEN

"Let Education Open a Door"

Amal David, born a Palestinian, now a naturalized American citizen, is department head of bilingual programs at Detroit's Southwestern High School, which has about a forty-percent Arab-American student enrollment. Many of the students are from recently immigrated families where Arabic is still the main language spoken in the home. Under Amal's direction, the Arabic language is used along with English to make teaching most effective.

When Amal came to the United States in 1970, she was herself only a high school graduate. She was born in Nazareth, which, by the time she finished high school,

Amal David teaches recent Arab and other immigrants in Detroit's Southwestern High School.

was part of the West Bank territory occupied by Israel in the 1967 war. "None of my sisters had gone to college," Amal said, "but I wanted to go. I wanted to study in the United States, and I was able to get a student visa to go there.

"I was raised in a Catholic family by protective parents, and they did not want me to go to a strange country by myself. It took me two years to persuade them to let me come and only then after a missionary was able to help me get into Lubbock Christian College, a strict Church of God school in Texas.

"At first I had a terrible time with English at Lubbock Christian. I thought I knew English well, but they do

103

not speak it in Texas as they do in Nazareth. And I thought I would be disgraced if I did not make an A in every subject. In the end I did well, but I almost had a nervous breakdown. And I was so poor. I had to work to make ends meet. During the summers I sold Bibles door to door! You try that sometime. It will help your English, and it will help you know Americans.

"I received a Bachelor's degree in education at Lubbock Christian, and then I was accepted for graduate work at Michigan State University. I earned a Master's degree in communications there and then went to Ohio State University to work on a doctorate. I received my Ph.D. degree from Ohio State in 1982, also in communications. My dissertation was a study of Arab stereotypes in social-studies textbooks.

"Between degrees I returned to Nazareth. I am not sure whether I thought I would stay there or whether I meant it to be just a visit. But after I had been there only a short time, I knew I could not stay. I had changed too much. There you must be a conformist. You must not question authority. I am proud to be an Arab, but it was difficult to be proud in the West Bank. My father and mother saw how much I had changed. They both said to me, 'You must go back to America.'

"And so I returned to stay. I became a citizen. I married a third-generation Arab American. He does not speak Arabic, but in some way he is more Arab than I am. We have two lovely little girls, and he insisted that they have Arab names. One is Zayna, which means beautiful; the other is Ameera, which means princess.

"I am so happy here in America. I can express myself politically without fear. I have a good job at Southwestern High School. I can breathe.

"There are problems, of course. You know that my Ph.D. dissertation was about Arab stereotypes in the United States. Sometimes it is scary—the amount of misinformation about Arabs and hostile feelings toward them. Just last week a woman—a teacher—said to me, 'I can't stand Arab culture.' I asked her why and she said, 'The way they treat women. Arab women have to walk behind their husbands. They aren't allowed to do anything.'

"That is nonsense. There are places in the Arab world where women are still repressed. But Arab women have a great deal of power in the home, and their role is changing rapidly in a number of Arab countries. Today in the Middle East many Arab women are doctors, lawyers, scientists, teachers, managers. Hundreds of women from my city alone, Nazareth, are getting their education all over the world, many of them here in the United States, as I did. Many will return to the Middle East.

"The answer is education, at least part of the answer. It can open so many doors that would otherwise never be opened. That is what I tell my Arab-American students here in Detroit. Let education open a door for you."

Education has opened doors for many Arab immigrants and their descendants. Most early Arab immigrants to America came for economic opportunity. They found what they sought, and they made sure that their children took advantage of the educational opportunities that America offered. "If you don't use your brain, you're going to have to use your feet," Lebanese peddler and merchant Alexander Courie told his sons as he sent them off to college. A high percentage of second-, third-, and fourth-generation Arab Americans have gone to college and become doctors, lawyers, engineers, scientists, and teachers.

Dr. George Shadid, a dentist in Borger, Texas, comes from a family that originated in Lebanon. There are a large number of doctors and dentists in the Shadid family, spread all over the Southwest but mainly in Oklahoma and Texas. Speaking of Arab Americans in general, Dr. Shadid said to me, "All our families started here as peddlers and merchants. I guess later generations just wanted to show they could do things in the professions."

Like early Arab immigrants to America, many of those who came after World War II were motivated chiefly by the prospect of economic opportunity; others im-

Born in Kuwait, Munib Derhalli has lived most of his life in Portland, Oregon, where he is now a fourth-year dental student at the Oregon Health Sciences University. The fields of medicine and dentistry have attracted many Arab Americans.

migrated because of political dislocation and turmoil. Unlike early Arab immigrants, however, many young men and women from the Arab world—beginning in the 1960s and continuing to the present—have come to the United States primarily to begin or complete their college and university education. U.S. Immigration and Naturalization records indicate that almost eighty thousand student visas were issued to Lebanese and Jordanians (mostly Palestinians living in Jordan) between 1975 and 1988. The total number of student visas from all Arab countries is several times that figure.

107

Many early Arab immigrants to America planned to stay only a few years, make their fortune, and return to live in luxury in their original homeland. Most of them changed their minds, and America became their new homeland. This same thing has happened in the cases of thousands of young Arabs who have come in recent years to the United States to study. They have stayed in America and have become American citizens, either because of economic or professional opportunity or—particularly for Lebanese and Palestinians—because war and political turmoil have made their home a difficult or impossible place to return to.

Habib and Noel Yaziji. He is Syrian; she is Lebanese. Like so many Arabs, they came to the United States initially for an education and planned to return to Lebanon. Events in the Middle East changed their plans; they make their home in southern California, where both are teachers.

108

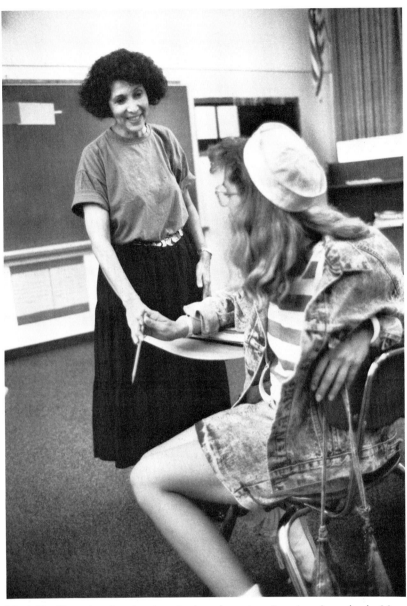

Noel Yaziji teaches hearing-impaired students in a Los Angeles suburb. Many Arab Americans, particularly Lebanese and Palestinians, have entered the teaching profession in the United States.

Mikhael Haidar, his wife Linda, and their three children live in a five-bedroom, one-hundred-year-old house in Walpole, Massachusetts, a suburb of Boston. Mikhael, an electrical engineer, and Linda have restored the house themselves. In every way they are a typical American suburban family except for one thing: Mikhael was born and raised in a village in Lebanon and until ten years ago never dreamed that he would spend his life in the United States.

"I didn't come to the U.S. as an immigrant," Mikhael told us. "I didn't come to stay. I came to this country for a simple reason. For anybody wanting to go to college, this is the land of education. It is also a place where

Linda and Mikhael Haidar (on each end) with their children and Mikhael's parents and sister.

you can work and study. I went to Northeastern University here in the Boston area. I financed my own education, working at two jobs and sometimes something on the side. One of my jobs was security guard at night. This regimen made me a better, stronger person."

Mikhael noted that the Lebanese civil war was a major reason for the large influx of Arab students to U.S. colleges. At the peak there were over four hundred Arab students at Northeastern University. Mikhael started the Arabic Club there, and it is still an active campus organization.

"I helped my cousins come to the U.S. to go to college," Mikhael said. "We all brought our cousins."

The village in which Mikhael grew up was fifteen miles from Tripoli in Lebanon's Alkoura region. It is an area of extremely high literacy and home to many professional people. "As long as history has been kept my family came from that village," Mikhael said. "My wife, Linda, is not an Arab, but she was prepared to go back with me. When we married we took it for granted that someday we would go there to live.

"But after I graduated in '78, there was nothing to go back to—because of the civil war. The choice then for engineers was either to stay here or go to Saudi Arabia to find a job. Our choice was to stay here."

We talked with Linda one night. "I liked the idea of acquiring an extended family," she said. "I have learned some Arabic at Harvard. We are trying to introduce our children to it. Their grandmother has told them so much about Lebanon that they are dying to go and play with their cousins. We talk about Mikhael's home regularly. Lots of letters come from the village, and we read portions to the children so they will have a sense of what Mikhael's past was like.

"As the children get involved in American society, it gets harder for them to leave," Mikhael said. "The same is true for me. I have so many community commitments. If a miracle happened and Lebanon was returned to normal, we might keep two homes and spend part of our life in each. The world is so small: travel is no problem. Lebanon is so close, and I would like to help in its rebirth. But if we went now, it probably would not be a permanent move. I am an American now, but I left a country that once was beautiful, and a part of me will always be sad."

Growing Up Arab American

"As kids we rejected our culture," Evelyn Menconi told us when we talked to her at the St. George Orthodox Church in the Boston suburb of West Roxbury. "My brothers and sisters and I wanted so much to be Americans. We wanted to be like all the other kids. We were ashamed of our Arab background. I wouldn't even put Arab food in my lunch box when I went to school."

Evelyn Menconi—her maiden name was Abdalah—grew up in the Boston area and has lived all of her life there. Her parents were born in Lebanon, came to America early in the twentieth century, and met and married in Boston. Evelyn's father first became a ped-

Evelyn Menconi

dler, then a clerk in a Boston store, later a store owner. Before coming to Boston to look for a job, her mother had worked in a nearby textile mill.

At that time in the century Boston had a larger Arab-American population than any other U.S. city except New York; but in this New England cradle of democracy, prejudice against recent immigrants was strong, and particularly strong against those who had come from parts of the world other than Europe. In *Taking Root, Bearing Fruit*, Evelyn Shakir quotes a Boston social worker of that time as writing, "Next to the Chinese, who can never be in any real sense Americans, the Syrians are the most foreign of all our foreigners. Whether on the street in their Oriental costumes or in their rooms

114

gathered around the Turkish pipe, they are always apart from us . . . and out of all nationalities would be distinguished for nothing whatever excepting as curiosities." To put such sentiments in context, Ms. Shakir points out that it was in Boston that the Immigration Restriction League was born in 1894.

Evelyn Menconi's mother was not one to be intimidated by such a hostile climate. She returned to Lebanon three times for visits during her life. She taught her children to read and write in Arabic. "But I forgot everything," Evelyn said, "and I forgot how to speak the language except for 'kitchen' Arabic. Later my mother insisted that I visit Lebanon to become familiar with the birthplace of my parents, to become acquainted with my roots."

Evelyn went to Lebanon in 1955 when the tiny country was still at peace. She visited relatives, experienced the hospitality of the people, saw the beauty of the ancient land. "The visit really opened my eyes," Evelyn told us. "I learned how stupid I had been. I began to realize what a strong and special people Arabs are and what a fine cultural heritage I have."

Today Evelyn Menconi is one of the most active persons in the Boston area in interpreting Arab culture and the Arab-American experience. Several years ago she started the William G. Abdalah Memorial Library, a collection of books about Arabs and Arab Americans, in memory of her brother. An educator all of her professional life, Evelyn takes a special interest in organizing school programs about Arab culture and Arab Americans. "It's not the same Boston I knew as a child," she said. "Now schools are interested in people with different backgrounds and different cultures."

One of Evelyn Menconi's major achievements in recapturing her cultural roots has been to learn Arabic. "That has been a beautiful experience for me," she said.

Many Arab Americans we talked with had gone through the same three-stage pattern or progression that Evelyn Menconi experienced: rejection of their Arab heritage as children, gradually coming to understand and accept it, and finally developing an intense pride in their cultural roots.

On the other hand, some of those we interviewed had positive feelings about growing up as part of an Arab-American family. When he told me about his years as a boy in Detroit and how he had enjoyed Arab music and dancing, Casey Kasem said, "I knew I was different, but it never bothered me. I liked being different, and my appearance and background helped in that way. I got a lot of support from my family. My mother always felt there wasn't anything I couldn't do. My grandmother was sure I would be famous someday—like Arthur Godfrey, she said."

Imam Talal Eid, shown here with his family, is religious director of the Islamic
Center of the Northeast in Quincy, Massachusetts, near Boston. Muslims in a
number of U.S. cities have established Islamic centers for religious, educational,
and community service programs. Some have full-time resident imams, who lead
prayers, solemnize weddings, conduct funerals, and supervise religious education.
Imam Eid was an imam in Lebanon before being assigned to Quincy in 1982 by
the Muslim World League.

*　　*　　*

Warren David was born in 1952 in Pawtucket, Rhode Island, a New England mill town to which many Arab immigrants were drawn earlier in the twentieth century. Warren's grandparents were born in Syria and Mount Lebanon; his paternal grandfather started his life in America as a peddler, his maternal grandfather as a worker in the Pawtucket textile mills.

"My last name should be Salloum, not David," Warren told us. "My paternal grandfather's name was David Salloum. But when he went for his citizenship papers, his last name had been put down as David. They told him it would cost a hundred dollars to have all the papers redone—which probably wasn't true—so he just let the mistake stand. He became Salloum David."

I asked Warren how he got his first name. "My father was a baseball fan," he said. "He named me for one of his favorite players, Warren Spahn, the great left-handed pitcher of the old Boston Braves."

As second-generation Arab Americans, Warren's mother and father Americanized quickly, adapting easily to the dominant culture. They prized their Syrian-Lebanese heritage, but to their children they spoke English.

"Except when they were mad at us," Warren said. "Then they used Arabic. I didn't learn to speak Arabic, but I can pronounce the names of all Arab foods perfectly, and I know some choice angry words."

118

Warren's parents were active in the Antiochian Orthodox Church, which had an almost exclusively Arab-American membership. Warren enjoyed the church's ethnic social events, the indoor *hasla*, the outdoor *marhajan*, parties with Arab music and dancing and lots of good festive food.

"And every year," Warren said, "there was a huge *marhajan* at Narragansett Race Track. Arab Americans came from all over. It was a chance for boys and girls to meet each other. Some of the girls changed their outfits four times a day."

Warren developed a great love of Arab music. A relative in Beirut sent him a *derbecki*, the Arab drum, which he learned to play. He became increasingly proficient and now regularly joins the musicians at Arab-American social events in Detroit, where he and his wife Amal live. He also began to collect records and tapes of Arab music and has one of the best private collections of such music in the United States.

I asked Warren if he had been aware of prejudice or discrimination against Arab Americans as he was growing up. "Not really," he said. "I was sometimes called camel jockey in school, but it was just joking, kids horsing around. I guess there were times when I felt a little like an outsider, when I was very much aware that I came out of a different cultural background than most of the kids in school. But mostly I enjoyed being who

I was. I think my parents felt more prejudice in their time. I remember my mother saying that she had been called a black Syrian. I didn't know what that meant, and I still don't. But I'm sure it wasn't meant to be complimentary."

It was in college, Warren said, that his Arab-American background really took on a new meaning and importance. He went to Ohio University, where there were many students from all parts of the Arab world. "It was exciting to meet them," Warren said, "to get to know people my age who had grown up in the land of my ancestors. I joined Arab student clubs at the university, became active in Arab student affairs. I decided I wanted to marry a woman from the Arab world. Meeting Amal, who was born in Palestine, in Nazareth, made that decision easy."

After college Warren and Amal settled in Detroit, where they quickly became involved in Arab-American activities, Amal as a bilingual teacher, Warren in media work focused on creating a better understanding of Arabs and Arab Americans. He now works in financial management.

I asked Warren why he thought being an Arab American had become so important in his life. "I'm not sure," he said. "People are different. I have a younger brother who grew up wanting to cut all ties to his Arab identity.

Warren David with his and Amal's daughters, Zayna and Ameera.

But to me it is a beautiful thing to know that I have a special culture and a cultural heritage."

For a girl growing up in an Arab-American family there can be special problems. At a 1989 Arab-American Anti-Discrimination Committee convention, a panel discussion was held on what it is like to grow up as an Arab American. One of the participants, Basma Rahim, spoke about the difference in the way that Arab-American parents treat their sons and daughters. She used her family—a Muslim family—as an example but suggested that they were typical of most Arab-American families,

121

at least of those in which the mother and father are first-generation immigrants.

Ms. Rahim talked about the unequal treatment of sons and daughters in her family, which immigrated from Iraq to Cleveland during the seventies. She and her sisters were expected to help with the housework, which included doing dishes and cooking. Her brothers were excused from such chores. That was a girl's job, their mother told them. The boys were allowed to date. The girls were not, and the parents refused to discuss even the possibility. When the time came for college, the boys were permitted to consider schools outside Cleveland. The girls were restricted to Cleveland schools.

When Ms. Rahim pointed out to her mother that her older brother had been permitted to apply to college outside Cleveland, her mother replied, "*Howa waled*—He's a boy."

Howa waled became a joke between the sisters, Ms. Rahim said, but her need for independence was a very real thing. She had grown up most of her life in America, gone to school in Cleveland from the beginning, and had absorbed the concept of independence that she saw in her schoolmates. But on the subject of independence, her mother simply pointed out that they were Arabs and that just because other girls left home to go to college didn't mean that she should. But at least her parents gave her the freedom to choose what she would study in college. Ms. Rahim became an engineer.

In Portland, Oregon, Paul and I found evidence that the parentally imposed restrictions on Arab-American girls are not necessarily confined to Muslim families. In that city, which has a considerable Arab-American population, we met Laurice Alicia Azar—Laurie, as she is known to her family and friends. Laurie is twenty-four; she was born in Portland and is now a fitness instructor

Laurie Azar

at a local YMCA, working with people who have physical disabilities. Her parents are first-generation immigrants from Syria; a large number of her extended family, including her grandparents, live in Portland. Her family is Christian, belonging to the Antiochian Orthodox Church. Both Arabic and English are spoken in the family, and the main diet is Arab food. Laurie is the oldest of four children and the only one who is fluent in Arabic.

"I was the first grandchild," Laurie said, "and Arabic was all I heard as a baby. Until I was four or five, Arabic was all that I spoke. Now, with my parents I use both Arabic and English. I have a tendency to speak Arabic more with my mom than my dad. He's an engineer and speaks English in his work, of course.

"I feel fortunate that I have two languages because I can communicate with the older generation, like my grandparents. We're a tight-knit family. If I don't see my grandparents at least once a week, something is wrong. My siblings didn't get quite as concentrated a dose of Arabic as I did. In other words, our family has Americanized more as time went on. But my roots are very important because they are what I am. My heritage gives me a sense of who I am. I'd like to go back to where my parents were born. We've been planning a trip for three or four years, but it always falls through. I want to see how my family back there lives."

Speaking of the traditional nature of her family, Laurie said, "My parents are strict. They don't like for me to date. Sometimes I feel more Arab than anything else, but I was born in America. I am an American, and my parents have to understand that. At the same time, I respect them and want them to know my friends and whom I'm with. Marrying an Arab is not a necessity to me, but my parents would prefer it. I do want their approval."

Like many young Arab-American women, Laurie is a product of two cultures. Her challenge is to find the way to live happily and successfully within both. A phrase we heard several times in talking with young Arab Americans was that they were "caught between two worlds." Our Detroit friend, Terry Ahwal, had solved the dilemma in a very decisive way. "I take the best of both cultures," she said. That surely is not easy, but we are certain that many young Arab Americans are doing just that.

When we met Sarah Rask, Laurie Azar's cousin, we had a clear example of how much difference a generation or two can make. They are almost the same age—Sarah is twenty-three—both born in Portland within a year of each other. But Sarah's father, Paul Rask, is a third-generation Arab American, himself born in Portland. The Rask family is still very much aware of its Arab roots, but it has thoroughly melded into American cul-

Sarah Rask

ture. Sarah has a degree of independence unknown to Laurie.

"She can do anything she wants," Sarah's father told us, "as long as she doesn't embarrass herself or her family."

Sarah is proud of her background. "My maternal grandfather came here around the turn of the century," she said. "He dug ditches and eventually had his own construction company. He built the Lloyd Center here in Portland. My grandmother died two years ago at the

126

age of ninety-two. She was a schoolteacher and played soccer in Syria, where her father was the village mayor. She was well educated, very well respected, fun to be around. She was my idol. For a woman of her time, she was very liberated."

Sarah is aware that her ties to Arab culture are much less strong than Laurie's. "Unfortunately, I don't know any Arabic," Sarah said. "My mother bakes bread and makes other Arabic dishes—mainly, I think, to impress our friends—and even though I would like to continue that tradition, I really prefer hamburgers.

"I do have a strong sense of extended family. I have a bond with my cousins. Some of them are distant. We don't speak often, but I do feel close to them. My closest friends are my five brothers and sisters. All of us live here in Portland." Then Sarah used the same words that Laurie had used: "Something is wrong if we don't gather at least once a month."

Sarah is a senior at Portland State University majoring in communications. After she graduates, she wants to work in public relations.

Early in this century Arab immigrants to America were mostly young single men. Even if a male Arab immigrant had a wife and children, he seldom brought them to America until he was well established in this country; that often was a matter of years. Today the pattern of immigration has broadened. While many Arab immigrants to America are still single young men and women, the arrival of whole families from the Arab world is now a common occurrence.

There are several reasons for this change. Most persons immigrating from Arab countries already have one or more relatives in the United States who can sponsor them, thus making their entry easier. Also, a major motive for immigration in recent years has been to get families out of areas where war and political violence are serious threats. Airplane travel has made it possible for a family to leave the Middle East and arrive in America a few hours later; the same trip in the first decades of the century would have taken weeks or months and usually would have involved travel on two or more ships.

Every year, now, many Arab families with young children board commercial aircraft in Beirut, Jerusalem, Baghdad, or Cairo and arrive at busy U.S. airports. For Hesham Haj Yousif the port of entry was O'Hare Airport in Chicago. The year was 1969, and Hesham was four years old, one of six Yousif children whose ages ranged from three months to nine years. Immigration for the family had been possible because a relative in Chicago had sponsored them, and another relative in Georgia had paid their airfare.

The decision by Hesham's father to uproot his family and bring them to America had not been an easy one.

Originally from Ramallah in the land that had been Palestine, Dr. Yousif and his wife had immigrated to Kuwait after the 1956 war between Israel and the Arabs. Dr. Yousif had taken a position as one of the Emir of Kuwait's personal physicians. All the Yousif children were born in Kuwait.

The family might have lived there permanently in relative wealth and comfort, but Hesham's father had fought in two Arab wars against Israel, in 1948 and 1956; now there was border fighting between Kuwait and Iraq, both Arab countries. With immigration to the United States possible because of his relatives there and because his profession as a physician gave him preferred immigrant status, Yousif decided that the time had come to take his family out of the strife-torn Middle East.

Hesham's father was never able to practice medicine in America, because his English was not good enough for him to pass the qualifying examinations. There was no opportunity to study because the family had to be provided for. Both Yousif and his wife went to work for Western Electric in Chicago, both working double shifts and barely overlapping so one parent could stay with the children. They lived in a small apartment in a depressed area with a large Polish and Lithuanian population. The six children slept in one room on two beds.

After four years the Yousifs had saved enough money

to start a grocery store on a partnership basis with a relative. The store was not a success, but the Yousifs salvaged enough money from it to start a restaurant. That was more successful, and after a few years they bought a candy store, which, since it was located near a school, did a good business. The restaurant and the store were entirely family businesses. Either the mother or the father, and usually both, were there at all times. From the time he was six, Hesham worked in the restaurant when he was not in school.

School in this tough part of Chicago was not easy. When he began first grade, Hesham knew almost no English, but he learned quickly enough what such phrases as "dirty Arab" and "camel jockey" meant.

Hesham Haj Yousif

"The kids pronounced it 'A-rab,' " Hesham said. "I was a dirty A-rab." It got worse in 1973, when the Middle East oil embargo caused gasoline prices to sky-rocket. "I got into lots of fights, and so did my brothers," Hesham said. "Newspapers and television were full of stories about how Middle East countries were ruining America by raising oil prices. Arab-American kids in school were easy targets."

Today Hesham is studying law at American University in Washington, D.C. Although he still speaks Arabic, his English is flawless and without a trace of accent. His interest in his Arab heritage is deep, and his ambition is to go into international law focused on the Middle East. He is unhappy with Arab countries and Arab religious groups for their bitter enmities that have kept the Middle East in turmoil. He is unhappy with America for its ignorance of the tragedy of the Palestinians that is behind much of the Middle East friction.

While Hesham understands and agrees with the precepts of Islam, he is not himself a practicing Muslim. Had he grown up in Kuwait, he doubtless would have been. But since he grew up in Chicago, where there were no mosques or deep Islamic traditions, where Islamic teaching and ritual were not a part of the schools he went to, the Muslim religion did not become an integral part of Hesham's life.

*   *   *

Young Arab Americans at confirmation services, Saint Nicholas Orthodox Cathedral, Los Angeles.

132

Hesham is far from the exception in terms of the diminishing role that Islam plays in his life. In Los Angeles we talked with Dr. Maher Hathout, who is chairman of the Islamic Center of Southern California. According to Dr. Hathout, studies have indicated that as many as eighty percent of the children of Muslim families that immigrate to the United States eventually leave Islam. Dr. Hathout hastened to point out that he was not speaking just about Arabs but rather about all Muslim immigrants, whatever their nationality or ethnic background: Pakistanis, Filipinos, Indonesians, Malaysians, among many others.

Keeping young Muslims close to their religion is clearly a priority for Muslim leaders. Dr. Hathout, who immigrated from Egypt to the U.S. in 1960, is in professional life a specialist in internal medicine and cardiovascular diseases. But the day we met him, he was preparing to take part in a three-day spiritual and educational retreat for young Muslim men and women of the Los Angeles area. Many of the sessions at the retreat would be devoted to prayer and study of the Koran, but some would be on such subjects as "Why Am I a Muslim?" and "Everything You Wanted to Know about Islam but Were Afraid to Ask."

Dr. Hathout said with some satisfaction: "This is the third year for the retreat. The first year we had sixty young people, the second year one hundred twenty.

Muslim children studying Arabic at the Islamic Center of Southern California.

This year we will have three hundred."

Speaking of the Islamic Center of Southern California, which serves about ten thousand families, Dr. Hathout said, "We at the Center are very keen to stress that we are first of all Americans. We are American Muslims. This is not a nostalgic mosque. It is part of America, not part of Cairo or Karachi. We are fanatically against taking financial aid from any government. That has made us free of outside control. We owe nothing to anyone but God."

*　　*　　*

134

In the Los Angeles suburb of Cerritos, we spent a pleasant evening with an Arab-American family in which the children are as deeply committed to Islam as the parents. Dr. Wasfy Shindy is chief of the Environmental Toxicology Laboratory of the County of Los Angeles. His wife, Nabila, was a high-school biology teacher for fifteen years; now she is director of a preschool with an enrollment of one hundred children. Their son, Waleed, is a senior in biology at UCLA, who plans to go on to medical school. Their daughter, Tammy, is also a student at UCLA.

Wasfy Shindy came to the United States from Cairo as a student in 1962 and received his Ph.D. degree in agricultural chemistry from the University of California at Davis in 1969. Waleed was born in 1967, Tammy in

The Shindy family

1968, while the Shindys were still at Davis. "Initially I intended to go home after I finished my studies," Dr. Shindy told us. "In Egypt, with my Ph.D. from the University of California, I would have been a big fish. Here in America I'm a small fish in a big tank. Here I'm just an ordinary guy. But I liked American life, and we decided that our children would have a better future here than they would in Egypt. So we stayed."

Dr. Shindy is perhaps modest in his characterization of himself as "an ordinary guy." In his position as chief of the Environmental Toxicology Laboratory, he is directly concerned with the health of the entire population of Los Angeles County. "I check everything," he said, "the water we drink, the food we eat. We monitor everything to check levels of toxic chemicals. We try to head off disaster before it occurs. We solve problems without letting people know a problem even existed. Right now we are checking drinking fountains in public schools for lead concentration. We can monitor two hundred seventy-five different chemicals. Much of the time I am a scientific detective."

The entire Shindy family holds strictly to the tenets of Islam. They pray five times each day. They observe the fasting month of Ramadan. They attend a mosque regularly. They observe the restrictions on food and drink. "Here," Dr. Shindy said, "Muslim parents must raise their children to be even better Muslims than do people in Egypt. Only by adhering to the strictest standards will your children keep their Muslim identity. Otherwise, they will drift away from their religion, from Islam."

Waleed is active in the Muslim Youth Council of the Islamic Center of Southern California and has helped to organize all the Muslim youth retreats. He agrees with his father about the importance of adhering strictly to Muslim tradition. "In order to keep our Muslim and Arab identities," he said, "we have to look toward our own community. Cultural obstacles in a mixed marriage could very easily pose problems. We have known mixed marriages that don't work. I have made my choice to marry an Egyptian Muslim girl."

Young Muslims attending a youth retreat near Los Angeles. Some of those attending are Arab Americans, but many come from non-Arabic backgrounds.

I asked Tammy about the problems of growing up as a Muslim girl—dressing modestly, not dating—in a big California high school. "Being a Muslim in high school was not a problem," she said. "Many of my classmates were Orientals who came from very strict, conservative families. They understood."

Both Tammy and Waleed regret that they cannot read Arabic.

"I feel a great void in my heart because I have to read the Koran in English," Waleed said. "I would like to see my children not experience the same void."

The Southern Maryland Islamic Center in Prince Frederick, Maryland, was built in 1984 at the urging of Iraqi-born doctor Issam Dmalouji. Dr. Dmalouji is chief of the medical staff at Calvert Memorial Hospital (just across the street from the mosque). The mosque has about forty members.

A Friday noon service at the Southern Maryland Islamic Center.

"I have to learn it because I want to teach my children," Tammy said.

Dr. Shindy is optimistic about the future. "I believe that Islam will flourish in the United States," he said. "Here we can practice our religion more freely than we would be able to in several Arab countries with factional conflicts. There are no restrictions here."

"We do suffer from stereotyping, though," Waleed said. "Now people think Arab-Muslim-terrorist. I want them to think Arab-Muslim-lawyer-doctor."

* * *

In 1926, the poet Kahlil Gibran, writing in a New York newspaper called *The Syrian World*, sent this message to young Syrian Americans:

I believe in you, and I believe in your destiny. I believe that you are contributors to this new civilization.

I believe that you have inherited from your forefathers an ancient dream, a song, a prophecy, which you can proudly lay as a gift of gratitude upon the lap of America.

I believe you can say to the founders of this great nation, "Here I am, a youth, a young tree whose roots were plucked from the hills of Lebanon, yet I am deeply rooted here, and I would be fruitful."

And I believe that you can say to Abraham Lincoln, "The blessed Jesus of Nazareth touched your lips when you spoke, and guided your hand when you wrote; and I shall uphold all that you have said and all that you have written."

I believe that you can say to Emerson and Whitman and James, "In my veins runs the blood of the poets and wise men of old, and it is my desire to come to you and receive, but I shall not come with empty hands."

I believe that even as your fathers came to this land to produce riches, you were born here to produce riches by intelligence, by labor.

And I believe that it is in you to be good citizens.

And what is it to be a good citizen?

It is to acknowledge the other person's rights before as-

serting your own, but always to be conscious of your own.

It is to be free in thought and deed, but it is also to know that your freedom is subject to the other person's freedom.

It is to create the useful and the beautiful with your own hands, and to admire what others have created in love and with faith.

It is to produce wealth by labor and only by labor, and to spend less than you have produced that your children may not be dependent on the state for support when you are no more.

It is to stand before the towers of New York, Washington, Chicago and San Francisco saying in your heart, "I am the descendant of a people that builded Damascus, and Biblus, and Tyre and Sidon, and Antioch, and now I am here to build with you, and with a will."

It is to be proud of being an American, but it is also to be proud that your fathers and mothers came from a land upon which God laid his gracious hand and raised His messengers.

Young Americans of Syrian origin, I believe in you.

More than fifty years after Kahlil Gibran's message, Paul and I crossed the United States, talking to young Arab Americans such as Terry Ahwal, Laurie Azar, Amal and Warren David, Sarah Rask, Tammy and Waleed Shindy, and Hesham Yousif. I feel very sure that Kahlil Gibran, were he here today, would write the same message that he wrote in 1926.

141

Bibliography

Abraham, Sameer Y., and Nabeel Abraham, eds. *Arabs in the New World*. Detroit: Center for Urban Studies, Wayne State University, 1983.

Ashabranner, Brent. *Gavriel and Jemal: Two Boys of Jerusalem*. New York: Dodd, Mead & Company, 1984.

Caldwell, Tom Joe. "The Syrian-Lebanese in Oklahoma." Norman, Okla.: Master's thesis, University of Oklahoma, 1984.

Kamm, Antony. *The Story of Islam*. New York: Cambridge University Press, 1987.

Kurtz, Howard. "Arab Americans in New York Say Mayoral Nominees Spurn Support." *The Washington Post*, October 16, 1989.

Lamb, David. *The Arabs: Journeys Beyond the Mirage*. New York: Random House, Inc., 1987.

Mansfield, Peter. *The Arab World: A Comprehensive History.* New York: Thomas Y. Crowell, 1977.

Milloy, Courtland. "Jews, Arabs Hold Dinners for Peace." *The Washington Post*, March 8, 1986.

Morris, Benny. *The Birth of the Palestinian Refugee Problem, 1947–1949.* New York: Cambridge University Press, 1988.

Muslih, Muhammad Y. *The Origins of Palestinian Nationalism.* New York: Columbia University Press, 1988.

Naff, Alixa. *The Arab Americans.* New York: Chelsea House Publishers, 1988.

Orfalea, Gregory. *Before the Flames: A Quest for the History of Arab Americans.* Austin, Tex.: University of Texas Press, 1988.

Regan, Geoffrey. *Israel and the Arabs.* New York: Cambridge University Press, 1989.

Ross, Frank, Jr. *Arabs and the Islamic World.* New York: S. G. Phillips, 1979.

Shipler, David K. *Arab and Jew: Wounded Spirits in a Promised Land.* New York: Times Books (a division of Random House, Inc.), 1986.

Weekes, Richard V., ed. *Muslim Peoples: A World Ethnographic Survey.* Westport, Conn.: Greenwood Press, 1984.

Zogby, James, ed. *Taking Root, Bearing Fruit: The Arab-American Experience.* Washington, D.C.: The Arab-American Anti-Discrimination Committee, 1984.

Index

Abourezk, James, 77–78
Abraham, F. Murray, 7
Abraham, Joseph, 18–19
Abraham, Dr. Nabeel, 74–75
Afranji, Frank and Lona, 75–76
Ahwal, Terry, 1, 50, 51–54, 75, 82, 83, 125
Al-ayubi, Lamees, 70–71
American Israel Public Affairs Committee, 74
Antiochian Orthodox Church, 22
Aossy, William, Sr., 25
Arab-American Anti-Discrimi-
nation Committee, 2–3, 53–54, 78, 121
Arab American Institute, 78
Arab Americans
cities with greatest concentration of, 42–43
desire for education, 107–8
number of in United States, 8
as peddlers in early days, 25–29
prejudice and discrimination against, 2–3, 6–7, 53–54, 76–79, 84–85, 130–31

Arab immigration to United States. *See* immigration.
Arabs
  contributions to human knowledge by, 13–14
  early history of, 10–11, 13–15
  modern definition of, 16
  traditional characteristics of, 10–11
Arab world
  countries of, 35
  wealth and poverty in, 39–40
Assed, Norman, 76–77
Awde, Halim, 86–91
Awde, Lebebe, 86, 87, 90–91
Azar, Laurice Alicia, 123–25

Beirut, 23
Bristow, Okla., 17–20

Courie, Alexander, 29–32, 106
Courie, Dr. Wadie, 29–32

Dajani, Nahida Fadle, 70–74
David, Amal, 102–6, 120
David, Warren, 118–21
Dearborn, Mich., 43, 46, 47, 48, 49
DeBakey, Dr. Michael, 7
Derhalli, Munib, 107
Detroit, Mich., 43–46
Dmolouji, Dr. Issam, 138

Druze (Islamic sect), 22–23, 70

Eastern Orthodox Church. *See* Antiochian Orthodox Church.
Eid, Imam Talal, 117

Gibran, Jean, 101
Gibran, Kahlil (sculptor), 93–101
Gibran, Kahlil (writer/poet/artist), 93, 99, 140–41

Haidar, Linda, 110, 111
Haidar, Mikhael, 110–12
Hathout, Dr. Maher, 133–34
Hindi, Moneer and Rasmie, 28
Hitti, Phillip K., 21
Houmaye, Saleh, 45

immigration of Arabs to United States
  beginnings, 21–24
  increase since 1965, 40–41
  restrictive law of 1924, 34
Iraqi invasion of Kuwait, 54–55
Islam
  origins of, 12
  spread of, 13, 15
  tenets of, 12
Israel
  creation of, 36–37

Arab wars since 1947
    against, 38

Jackson, Jesse, 6
Jerusalem, 37, 38
Jews (American), 74–77
Jordan, 37, 56
Joseph, Kadar, 27

Kasem, Casey, 3–7, 81, 116
Khoury, Malik, 19
Khudairi, Karim and Sajida,
    60
Kinston, N.C., 30, 31
Koran, 12
Kuwait invaded by Iraq, 54–55

Lahaj, Mary, 80
Lebanon
    civil war, 38–39
    religious diversity, 22–23
Lightner, Candy, 7
Livonia, Mich., 1, 2

Maronite (Christian sect), 22
Martha, Charlie, 85–86
Martha, Farideh Abu, 50, 85
Martha, Joe, 82–86
Martha, Rozette, 83
Martha, Shuchry (Chuck), 84–
    85
Martha, Zezette (Tootsie),
    85–86
McAuliffe, Christa, 7

Melkite (Christian sect), 22
Menconi, Evelyn, 113–16
Middle East Cousins Club of
    America, 81
Mikwee, Khalil, 26
Mitchell, Senator George, 7
Mount Lebanon, 21–25
Muhammad, 11–13
Mullens, W.Va., 64, 66

Nader, Ralph, 7
Naifeh, Ed, 19
Najjar, Dr. Abdallah E., 62–
    70
Najjar, Jean, 63, 66
New Orleans, 59

Ottoman Turks, 22–23

Palestine, 36–37, 79
Palestinians
    diaspora, 37–38
    as refugees, 38
    statelessness of, 79

Rahim, Basma, 121–23
Ramallah, 1, 51, 83
Rask, Paul, 125, 126
Rask, Sarah, 125–127

Shadid, Anthony, 2–3
Shadid, Dr. George, 106
Shakir, Evelyn, 114
Shalhoub, Fr. George, 2

Shatila, Riad, 43
Shibley, Warren, 19
Shiite (Muslim sect), 22
Shindy, Nabila, 135
Shindy, Tammy, 135–139
Shindy, Waleed, 135–139
Shindy, Dr. Wasfy, 135–139
Siblani, Osama, 54–55
Siegel, Ellen, 79, 81
Srour, Merhaj, 91–93
Suleiman, Ahmad, 55–61
Sunnite (Muslim sect), 22
Sununu, John, 7
Syria, 21–22

Taking Root, Bearing Fruit
(Evelyn Shakir), 114–15

Washington Area Jews for Israeli-Palestinian Peace,
79
West Bank, 1, 56

Yaziji, Habib, 108
Yaziji, Noel, 108, 109
Yousif, Hesham Haj, 128–
31

Zobgy, James, 78